BEING OF TWO MINDS

BEING OF TWO MINDS

THE VERTICAL SPLIT IN
PSYCHOANALYSIS AND PSYCHOTHERAPY

Arnold Goldberg

THE ANALYTIC PRESS

1999   Hillsdale, NJ   London

Published by
The Analytic Press, Inc.
Editorial Offices:
101 West Street
Hillsdale, New Jersey 07642

Designed and typeset by Compudesign, Rego Park, NY
Index by Leonard S. Rosenbaum

Library of Congress Cataloging-in-Publication Data

Goldberg, Arnold, 1929–
    Being of two minds : the vertical split in psychoanalysis and psychotherapy / Arnold Goldberg
        p.   cm.
    Includes bibliographical references and index.
    ISBN 0-88163-308-9
    1. Multiple personality—Case studies. 2. Dissociative disorders—Case studies. I. Title.
    [DNLM: 1. Dissociative disorders case studies.
    2. Personality disorders—Case studies. 3. Psychoanalytic Therapy case studies. WM 173.6 G618b 1999]
    RC569.5M8G65 1999
    616.85'236—dc21
    DNLM/DLC
    for Library of Congress   9833349
                                                                      CIP

Printed in the United States of America

10   9   8   7   6   5   4   3   2   1

To my analytic teachers:

Joan Fleming, Roy Grinker, and Heinz Kohut

CONTENTS

ACKNOWLEDGMENTS

Over time I am sure that I have learned so much from so many that it is impossible for me to acknowledge all of my debts. I take comfort in having been a perpetual student surrounded by willing teachers. However, I owe much to Dr. Jan Fawcett who, as chairman at Rush-Presbyterian-St. Luke's Department of Psychiatry, has supported me in more ways than I can readily list. A group of colleagues and friends—Harvey Freed, Mark Gehrie, Robert Gordon, Sheldon Meyers, Caryle Perlman, Brenda Solomon, David Solomon, Jeffrey Stern, and Ruth Yanagi—read and commented on much of my original manuscript. The many residents in Rush's psychiatry department over the years have had to listen to me go on about the vertical split, and I thank them all for their patience and wakefulness. Ms. Christine Susman remained my usual, available selfobject who also types.

Portions of chapter 7 were published in *The Psychoanalytic Quarterly* and much of the final chapter was my plenary address to the American Psychoanalytic Association. Paul Stepansky is felt by many to be the ideal editor and publisher. I enthusiastically join that group.

The fact that the goddess of truth who leads Parmenides places him before two paths, that of discovering and that of concealment, signifies nothing other than the fact that *Dasein* (human being) is always already both in the truth and the untruth. The path of discovering is gained only in distinguishing between them understandingly and in deciding for the one rather than the other.

Martin Heidegger

BEING OF TWO MINDS

PART I

THE SPLIT

Chapter 1

INTRODUCTORY REMARKS

The morning paper tells a story of a prominent man caught in an embarrassing and compromising position. The radio announces that a Hollywood star has been arrested for shoplifting. In case after case we hear of persons who, although they may not be actors in scenarios quite as dramatic as that of Dr. Jekyll and Mr. Hyde, do seem to have secret or unwholesome other lives. Sometimes these individuals initially deny but then reluctantly admit these other hidden parts of themselves. Sometimes they claim that they themselves cannot begin to comprehend why they do what they do. All too easily, the public condemns or is shocked to learn about incidents of delinquent, criminal, or immoral behavior in people who are held up as otherwise moral and even admirable. A good number of these individuals reveal a severe and striking split in their personalities, a vertical split in which side-by-side individuals seem to reside in but one mind. By the use of the word *split*, I mean a significant division of the organization of the personality into a divided pair. The division is not always neat, and the parts are never equal either in frequency of emergence or length of stay, but the experience for the person is one of a separation: a parallel and coexisting other.

Consider a reasonably financially secure woman who finds herself stealing food in the supermarket. She feels both compelled to do it and also horrified that she does it. She says it is as if another person took charge and accomplished the deed, leaving her to deal with the aftermath. The "as if" of another person, however, is always a problem, inasmuch as she also knows and feels it was she. She can neither comprehend nor explain her behavior. This, then, is the split.

This book is an effort to explain and understand that split in psychoanalytic psychological terms and by way of psychoanalytic theory. We shall comprehend this psychological state as a pathological one, a symptom of a disorder rather than a moral failing. I will extend this explanation to encompass a variety of similar psychological symptoms and so aim to raise our consciousness as to the far-ranging prevalence of this vertical split.

This work is a companion volume to an earlier one on the problem of thinking about and treating perverse sexual activity (Goldberg, 1995). Since that book's publication, the perversions have been renamed and turned by the American Psychiatric Association into the paraphilias (implying preference rather than pathology), and the ideas presented in the book have been extended into a wider net. The resultant larger picture includes an extensive range of behavior disorders similar to perverse behavior, but usually dealing with the substitution of an activity other than the sexual. Thus, misbehavior such as seen in eating disorders, delinquencies, and other ordinarily offensive or forbidden ways of life make up the group. The common element that holds this group together is this split in the personality, which allows the coexistence of the normal alongside the deviant. Once one gets a clear comprehension about this split, it begins to take on a life of its own, and soon it starts to be seen almost everywhere. After this initial burst of excited enthusiasm, a pullback to reason allows a more careful categorization of the split into the four groups that are presented in this book. That grouping consists of (1) circumscribed dissociation, (2) narcissistic personality disorders, (3) narcissistic behavior disorders, and (4) multiple personality disorders, the last being discussed with no representative clinical illustrations. The vertical split is expanded from its significance in the book on perverse behavior to its more general application.

This detailed discussion of the vertical split begins with an effort to define it and show its occurrence in certain selected case examples. The first chapter is designed to distinguish the vertical split from the number of other similar problems, ranging from ambivalence to repression, or the horizontal split. This is followed by a chapter that focuses on the major structural problems in this split: a failure of synthesis or integration in a self that becomes and remains divided.

The main theme in understanding the development of the vertical split is that these different forms derive from a childhood in which such splitting was a necessary part of existence. The parental directions given to the child, both explicitly and implicitly, demanded a division of one's personality into these side-by-side sectors. One cannot, of course, prove this assumption, but the case examples support it and may convince the reader of its likelihood. A chapter on parental collusion is followed by one on development, which is an effort to spell out in detail just how growing up in this environment allows this particular form of difficulty to emerge. The limitations of this chapter are inherent in any work on the choice of symptom and the degree of pathology. One can make some educated guesses but not much more; nevertheless the study of developmental issues is crucial in explaining the origin of these conditions.

The second part of the book is devoted to the treatment of the disorders associated with the vertical split. I start with a chapter that may initially seem unnecessary but is essential to working with some of these patients; this chapter concerns the issues of boundaries and commitment. The chapter that follows is a paradigmatic one that presents infidelity as one prevalent and familiar symptom of a vertical split found in many of our patients. This theme appears in a debate about socially acceptable versus socially condemned behavior characteristic of the split.

The specific treatment issues outlined in the ensuing chapter extend the main theme of the book in that the childhood and developmental origins of the split become reproduced in the transference. This reproduction is represented in a correlative and reciprocal manner in the transference. No doubt this will be the most controversial and problematic point of the book, inasmuch as it calls on therapists to struggle with a new version of the responses that patients evoke in us. The manner and method of addressing and working with this matched split between patient and therapist is the center of this chapter.

The four varieties of split mentioned earlier are showcased in the next chapter with illustrative case material that becomes either reintroduced or newly presented. Here multiple personality disorders are noted, but hardly anything crucial can be said about them owing to sheer lack of my clinical material. It remains a problematic and controversial topic.

The chapter on empathy and judgment is an effort to make some more general claims about the vertical split as it applies to themes that extend beyond those of our individual patients. The hope is that the concept does have more widespread application, and anticipates that more detailed studies will extend the concept to other arenas of interest. Once again the vision of the split becomes a part of our perception of events in the world at large and in our entire field of depth psychology.

The final chapter is filled with disclaimers. They are meant as markers or points of orientation to tell the reader that none of the present-day excursions and interests in psychoanalysis are being ignored or neglected in this old-fashioned type of book. A reprise of the experience of the split is used as the finale.

There are a number of cases presented, some at length and some briefly. Because they are all actual rather than fictionalized accounts, every effort has been made to disguise them as fully as possible. In the interest of disguise most of the cases are designated as male, although there was an equal gender distribution. After each disguising effort, another reader has been asked to make a further disguise. In a few cases and where possible, the permission of the patient has been obtained; several cases were discarded because permission was withheld. It is impossible to be absolutely certain that no confidentiality or privacy has been breached, and, short of writing entirely fictional reports, there seems no possible way that one can safely navigate between a duty to one's patients and a duty to our need to learn. I have done as well as I could.

Chapter 2

THE PROBLEM

Being of two minds is a state familiar to just about everyone who has had to make a choice between two equally appealing selections. The red or the blue, the pie or the cake, the one car or the other, elicit in us all of those conditions of an equal psychological balance or suspension that may even on occasion bring about pain and ultimately regret, as we come down on one side or the other. That experience of ambivalence or indecision begins with a choice that ordinarily has a similar or even identical endpoint in mind: the dessert should taste good, the car must drive well, and the color should be pleasing. This simple start, which contains the onset of ambivalence, takes a further significant step when the goals or aims resulting from the choices begin to separate and thus betray a significant difference between them. The cake versus the Jell-O has a different configuration of disparity, inasmuch as in deciding between cake and pie one cares not for calories whereas now one aims for some sort of dietary control. So, too, does the dilemma between the sedan and the convertible highlight a distinction between goals, ones that perhaps reflect a different lifestyle and an opposing overall presentation of one's image. Such differences begin to turn what is an ordinary run-of-the-mill ambivalence into more of a struggle between forces in opposition. Of course our supposedly simple ambivalence is made more complex because of whatever unconscious factors lay claim to one decision or another; if one adds together those unconscious determinants, which may traverse a wide range of wishes and fantasies, with the clear distinction between aims and goals, then we begin to approach a separation that seems to reflect two opposing personalities. So this further extension and elaboration of being of two minds results in more of a vertical separation, a division into side-by-side ways of thinking, or perhaps even one of personalities with differing aims, goals, and values.

No doubt almost everyone has had this sort of experience, in which coexisting feelings, which lead to different and opposite results, live within us. The struggle between eating heartily versus dieting effectively is but one example of a host of contradictory configurations that mark much of everyday life. It is not enough to say that one wants the one thing or the other, when one clearly and unambivalently wants both. And so preference often and regularly comes down to stilling the voice of the one, so that the other is not only heard but is allowed to dominate. The caloric overindulger must not listen to, must ignore, must literally deny, the claim to caloric control. She may do so momentarily or at length, but the denial or disavowal opens a gap or separation between these coexisting personalities; that is, the aim of one is temporarily the master of the mind while the other must take a holiday.

Most such vertical splits or separations are both innocent and short-lived. Indeed we all seem to have at times reckoned with these internal divisions because our goals are rarely both formed and clear, and so we may often struggle with divergent aims. The basis for this opposition lies sometimes, or perhaps usually, with our lack of clear and well-defined aims or values, such as the struggle between the pleasure of the moment and a commitment to longer-range goals. And, of course, these values stem from both conscious and unconscious principles of life and its direction. The simple virtues of honesty, beauty, fidelity, and so on, are always made more complex by the host of parental injunctions and prohibitions that come to compose other parts of our psyche (e.g., the superego). The same can be said about our personal expressions of how and when we find ourselves to be worthwhile and desirable individuals, and how we make choices with that in mind. But this struggle that takes place in many of us in its sometimes painful resolution of deciding upon one path or another is, for the most part, a struggle felt as such, and ordinarily is seen as residing in one person. That one person decides to do this or that, and the decision becomes owned by the same person. The short-lived split is resolved by the winning side claiming a victory over the entire person, and the losing side ceasing to clamor for attention and concern. It is only when we begin to see that victory does not always have a worthwhile resolution, and that neither side is able to tolerate losing, that we start to delineate a pathology. These splits of everyday life are not what we shall concern ourselves with in our consideration of the vertical split of pathology.

Perhaps the clearest presentation of the beginning pathology of disavowal and the concomitant vertical split can be seen in the complex patterns that followed the loss of an important relationship—a loved person or perhaps a pet animal—or even loss of a possession. The well-recognized denial that accompanies much of mourning work usually consists of various efforts at insisting that the loss has *not* occurred. From the occasional imaginary sighting of the lost object, on to the rarer maintenance of the room and possessions of the departed loved one, we see the range of efforts to undo the reality of the loss, to disavow what has been known to be true. This denial is usually and hopefully time-limited, as the bereaved individual proceeds through and by way of mourning to reinvest his or her interests elsewhere. It is rare to find the persistence of this denial of reality, and when that does happen, it is usually considered to qualify as a delusion. Indeed, it is the connection to an imaginary or unreal vision of the world that is said to cause a rent in the personality or ego of the person who cannot be committed to a single view of the world, but who finds it necessary to live in two worlds: sometimes simultaneously and sometimes sequentially. If one can, over time, reconcile oneself to a unitary vision of the world, then the grief is usually at an end. But until that time is reached, the psyche seems to move back and forth between one reality and another and, not surprisingly, it pays a heavy emotional price as long as this failure of reconciliation endures.

Persistent mourning may be rare, but other evidence of a personality that is divided, and remains lastingly so, is common. Before explicating the conditions that do reflect persistent separations, it is worthwhile to consider whether a unified or integrated self is ever to be taken for granted. The modern origin of unification goes back to René Descartes, who, although ordinarily thought of as a dualist in separating mind and body, also claimed that one's conscious awareness is the "I" or the person who observes and thinks about the world and so therefore exists as a unity. The undoing and effective demolition of that idea surely belongs to Sigmund Freud. Freud demonstrated a mental region that was not only not conscious but seemed to thrive in another place, with access available only under special circumstances and with special techniques. This separate part of the psyche conducted its affairs according to a different set of rules, and so it was claimed to be split off from the conscious arena; this was often illustrated by the use of a horizontal line called the repression barrier. The hoped-for unified self of Descartes was thus forever cleaved in two, and the effort to bring the disparate parts together was, in some eyes, seen as the fundamental work of psychoanalysis (i.e., to make the unconscious conscious). To now introduce a further exception, a vertical split as opposed to the horizontal one, demands a different kind of distinction between the two parts and a different form of psychoanalytic or psychotherapeutic work.

The ideational material or psychological contents that live behind the horizontal split or the barrier of repression are said to be actively withheld from consciousness. It is not ignorance that prevents a connection to this arena (Freud, 1927); rather, it is an active force that keeps it apart. Although some (Davidson, 1991) would claim that a form of conversation does exist between consciousness and the repressed, for the most part the unconscious is felt to connect and communicate in only the most devious ways, as in dreams, slips of the tongue, and transference. The contents of the vertically split-off segment seem different. Rather than being inaccessible, as the repressed is, one can attend to them, they are similar in form in the sense of being characterized as a secondary rather than primary process, and they manifest an organization reflecting a total personality. It is often only in respect to their relationship to the world that something different and even strange may be seen. For instance, in his discussion of fetishism (Freud, 1927), Freud held that the little boy had to cling to a bit of unreality—that of the existence of the little girl's penis—to form and maintain his split. Initially Freud joined repression to disavowal by maintaining that the idea was repressed while the affect was disavowed, but over time and throughout psychoanalytic history, as we shall see, there has been no easy solution to the relation of these two defensive operations. Suffice it to say that we now understand repression and disavowal to differ in development, construction, and content. But whereas the one—repression—seems to dominate the study of neuroses, the other—disavowal—seems to be of major significance in other forms of pathology. These latter conditions that center on disavowal seem most representative of the predicament with which we are concerned: that in which a person seems to inhabit two worlds.

To proceed past mourning to the pathological manifestations, perhaps the most outstanding example of this vertical split is found in the category of behavior disorders, which are characterized by a single individual behaving in seemingly contradictory ways. The honest teacher who sporadically steals books he may never read, the faithful housewife who regularly or irregularly picks up strange men in bars and goes to bed with them, the married heterosexual family man who visits gay bars and engages in furtive homosexual affairs, are all but a few of the examples of people who live parallel but contradictory lives, of people who seem to manifest evidence of being truly, at times, of two minds and so existing in two worlds. The split is striking in behavior disorders and less so in some of the other conditions that I will investigate. These behavior disorders primarily encompass the addictions including eating disorders, perversions, and delinquencies.

For the most part anyone who struggles with a repeated presence of a disparate part of himself or herself over time develops an attitude of either negative or tolerant or perhaps even positive valence toward its emergence. The honest and upright citizen despises his occasional foray into the men's washroom to pick up a young boy, the binge eater may have come to some sort of acceptance of her episodes of high-calorie sweets and the substance abuser may claim that all he desires is his fix as much as he regularly pledges to abstain. There is no predictable and regular reaction to one's parallel personality, nor can one ever be sure that any sort of attitude will carry the day. Sometimes the substance abuser does abstain, and sometimes the resolute bearer of virtue seems to give in all too easily to what he claims to abhor. Over time one may indeed discern a pattern for the emergence of what is, for some, a misbehavior. Not surprisingly, however, the real initiators of this misbehavior are elusive and so become subject to a series of rationalizations and excuses and even acceptance. Parallel, divided personalities often seem able to live with one another.

For Freud, the opposing set of thoughts and feelings was just that: opposite and demanding of opposition. The boy *had* vigorously to deny the possibility of castration by assigning a penis to the girl and so, of necessity, *had to* insist on truths that contradict. The failure of a unified vision is necessitated, and so all of the efforts to reconcile, to unify, are variations on the impossible. There is a fascinating neurological disorder called "alien hand" syndrome seen in patients who have had surgical severing of the corpus callosum, the structure that connects the two hemispheres, and in patients who have had anatomically similar brain damage from strokes or trauma. After surgery, for example, the patients feel that one hand is theirs and is owned by them, whereas the other feels foreign and alien. Indeed, this alien hand seems to have a life and will of its own, and its behavior seems not only to escape from the control of the person to whom it seems to belong, but it is more often at odds with the aims and intents of that person. An individual with a severed corpus callosum may struggle to keep the alien hand from doing or undoing something that the owned hand wishes to do. Sometimes the one hand holds down the other to keep it from a potential misbehavior. Although the patient so afflicted will tell you that he or she is clearly wanting and planning to perform a certain act, he or she seems as well to harbor a saboteur who is not heeding these directions and is bent on a different course.

One must, of course, be very cautious in claiming any one-to-one relationship between neurologic findings and those of psychological investigation, but a couple of authors (Levin, 1991; Basch, 1983) have suggested that one may indeed make such a connection between these disciplines in the explanation of disavowal and repression. One seems unable to escape the experience of duality, of contradiction that besets so many, and all sorts of explanations have been offered to determine its origin. As Montaigne (1588) says: "We are, I know not how, double in ourselves, so that we believe what we disbelieve, and cannot rid ourselves of what we condemn." The alien hand cannot be ignored or stilled. And yet, in some cases, it does seem—over time—to become absorbed by, or come under the control of, the person who once again feels that he or she is a unity. That process is usually without explanation, at least in the neurological sense.

Some of these disparate issues that range from the philosophic to the psychologic to the neurologic seem to come together in one patient's story of her struggle with what at times seemed to her to be an alien force within her. Her inner battle over eating was one such description of the conflict that occurs in persons who live with this sort of split.

Carol, one of our few female patients, has a long history of binge eating that of late is confined to periods when her husband is away on business. It begins this last time with a resolution of hers to limit herself to juices in order to lose weight. On the morning of this resolve, she launches this juice regime, but she finds herself famished by midmorning, and so the resolve is modified to include fruit as well. Some control is thereby relinquished. Over time more and more controls are established and abandoned, until she is fairly well gorging herself. This continues for a few days, until she plans to leave to join her husband. She tells of a dream that occurred before her departure. It features a man who is arguing vehemently with her and who seems in danger of falling from the staircase railing to which he holds. Despite the fury of his argumentative rage, Carol finds herself curiously aloof from his rantings, save for the fear that he might fall.

Carol leaves to join her husband, and the first night that they are together she dreams that she is pregnant, and she is terribly pleased that her stomach "feels like she has had but one meal rather than one hundred." Pregnancy makes her feel complete. Her associations to the dreams have to do with the arrogance of the man of the dream who seems both brilliant and out of control, and the feeling of pleasant satiation seems most clearly linked to the cessation of binging that arrives when she joins her husband. Now both dreams come together with herself as the onlooker as well as the out-of-control person whose eating seems propelled by a mixture of defiance and megalomania brought to a close by the presence of her husband, whom she sees as a nonsexual friend. Most of her lifelong sexual affairs that were intense were characterized by her being controlled by a tyrannical man, much like the man of the dream. She associates the bingeing with the sexual sphere, but bingeing is furtive and consists of an uncontrollable series of acts that occur when no man is present. Bouts of overeating began as a child but were always experienced as if happening to another person and were regularly followed by remorse and puzzlement. And now the vigorous argument of the dream and the previous conflicted sexual affairs seemed to mimic the arguments with her mother: the controlling tyrant of her childhood. Her mother is brought to life, and the fight begins anew. The dream is presented here only to illustrate this one facet of her struggle for control that so dominates her life.

Carol tells me of a fantasy she had while sitting in the waiting room for her appointment, which, on her request, had been changed to a new time and day. She imagined that another woman in the waiting room was prepared to be ushered into my office, and that I would emerge and be surprised at the presence of these two prospective and coscheduled patients. I would then proceed to ask the other woman to enter the office, while I explained to my patient Carol, according to her fantasy, that I had made an error and I would not be able to see her now. She would thereupon leave in a state of helpless rage at my being in control of everything. We discussed this fantasy both in terms of her perhaps wanting to avoid the hour and of her being guilty at getting a requested time. She insisted, however, that the focus of her feelings was the issue of control. All of the struggles as a child with her mother were those of control, and in all of them she saw the irrational position of her mother, and in all of them the mother won.

Carol saw a range of relationships with a variety of powerful (to her) people who exercised control over her, and who were equally unable to listen to or respect or believe her. Thus she routinely had to suffer the indignity of mistreatment at the hands of fools. From this picture of a relationship with another person, it was but a small step to the strange relationship that she had with herself when she binged on food. It always began with a fight over control, which she invariably lost. She was both victor and vanquished in this fight. And it always seemed to follow a loss or a separation. It was not so much that she became depressed, nor that now she was free to do as she pleased. The binge eating is restitutive. It restores her as she acts out a set of behaviors like the imagined argument in the waiting room. She is correct about the time, about reality, but the stronger person prevails. And indeed, whenever she looks back on a binge she can only feel that it had to do with another person, a foreigner whom she dislikes but who dominates her during these periods of excess. Carol says that she feels at times alien from herself, or as if she were someone else.

When we talk about her capacity to tolerate feelings, she insists that she has all sorts of feelings and indeed is beset by them. But she seems unable to tolerate any intense experience for very long. I suggest to her that her binge eating is a way for her to obliterate her feelings, and she immediately tells me a memory. She was saying good-bye to a friend and neighbor who lived in the same high-rise apartment building. Carol's apartment was on the fifth floor, and the friend's on the 14th. She recalls the profound sadness that she felt as, after the departure, the elevator descended these nine floors from her farewell to her friend to her own place. No sooner did she enter her apartment than she began to eat, and the depression disappeared. It was uncanny—just nine floors of sadness.

Here one can begin to see the elements that compose the problem of the two minds that seem at times to be like two persons. We must study and explain it not only as phenomenology, but we also have to make some effort to comprehend its origin, development, and structure, and ultimately propose some steps at amelioration or cure. The road from a conscious feeling of ambivalence to a painful experience of a set of warring internal forces is not a smooth one, and the most striking single point is the feeling of difference and alienation, of feeling as though one is split off from a stranger. There is no peace for someone to be as if two.

The struggle that is often the central point of unhappiness in people with behavior disorders is not easily comprehended by onlookers. Misbehavior of all sorts is too readily characterized as indulgence and weakness. The loss of control felt by persons who live with a split is easily joined to concepts such as childishness and pleasure-seeking and so becomes subject to moral condemnation. The customary response to this atmosphere of nonacceptance is concealment; the offending part of the personality is hidden from others as well as the self. This hiding is, however, only a partial and disguised effort and, somehow, somewhere, the split-off part manages to make itself known.

An Orientation to Perceiving the Split

. . . the truth has no need to be uttered to be made apparent, and (that) one may gather it with more certainty, without waiting for words and without even taking any account of them, from countless outward signs, even for certain invisible phenomena, analogous in the sphere of human character to what atmospheric changes are in the physical world. I might perhaps have suspected this, since it frequently occurred to me at that time to say things myself in which there was no vestige of truth, while I made the real truth plain by all manner of involuntary confidences expressed by my body and in my actions, . . . I ought to have suspected it, but to do so I should first have had to be conscious that I myself was occasionally mendacious and deceitful.

Marcel Proust (1933, p. 80)

When we talk to another person, we may well listen for nuances and emphases that suggest a subtext to the words that we hear, that is, we recognize that everything demands an interpretation of sorts. We do not regularly listen, however, as if there is another voice that would claim a hearing but is stilled. We expect a certain unity of presentation because that allows for a reasonable and unitary response. No one who asks for a cup of coffee is assumed to be simultaneously refusing one. Such a scenario leads only to paralysis. The psychoanalyst who infers the unconscious contents that lie behind the conscious ones is regularly dismissed if he or she chooses to respond to what is assumed but not spoken. Yet many do claim that a communication goes on outside of awareness, and some take it as central to their understanding of others.

The patient discussed previously began to live out her eating disorder in her treatment, but the overeater was not easily and readily a participant in the treatment. As we saw, some of this conflict was only hesitantly brought into the treatment. Inasmuch as this issue of being split off or split apart becomes a powerful one with these patients, it cannot be left to stay outside of the consulting room. We must next attend to how we are able to apprehend and comprehend the messages that are ordinarily anything but direct, because the split-off part is surely in attendance. Are they absent manifestly but inferred, or is it more likely that they are communicated in disguised or unusual form?

Psychoanalysis has always accepted the fact that unconscious communication does go on, but the explanation for it is not readily at hand. There is a need to better formulate the manner in which the two minds of the person can talk to the analyst, and just how the analyst can manage to make sense of this duality. Later it will become clear how this becomes a focal point for the treatment of the variety of conditions that manifest a vertical split.

The communication that is the object of study by psychoanalysts (i.e., what composes the messages exchanged by the patient and the analyst) has a tendency at times to take on something of a mystical or magical aura. In phrases and concepts such as "projective identification" there exists a presentation of a thesis that was surely derived from Freud's consideration of unconscious communication, that now claims that mysterious quantities, ideas, or feelings are passed from one person to another outside of the awareness of each participant. Either the patient projects or forces some set of thoughts and feelings into the analyst, or the analyst is able to know something and comprehend it without thinking about it, or some nascent elements of uncertain composition are given special symbols (Marcus, 1997). These elements are used to explain events otherwise not readily understood. The simple basis of overt verbal exchange along with covert contemplation of thoughts and feelings is felt to be insufficient to capture all of the sense of the communicative exchange and so these mysterious forces are introduced. This resort to arenas of study that seem to be at best pseudoscientific and at worst a retreat from efforts at more reasonable and rational explanations seems either to invite an abandonment of acceptable scientific standards or to be a form of special pleading familiar to the literature on ESP.

There is no doubt that one possible defense of this sort of discourse is to say that these explanations are only metaphoric expressions of events not easily explained by the usual comments about how persons communicate, but that they make no claim to any sort of actual or physical transmission of information. Thus a "projected identification" should not be taken to stand for anything substantial, any more than an "unthought known" (Bollas, 1987) really means anything more than a composite term for ideas that seem to exist outside of awareness. For example, Bion (1962) speaks of "raw experience" and "raw sense data" as being projected by a baby into a mother, and this process is then carried over into a similar transmission from patient to analyst. Marcus (1997) makes a case for analysts achieving a state that allows the patient's unconscious to communicate with the analyst's unconscious while both are unaware of what is transpiring, just as is said to transpire between baby and mother. The wholesale lumping of just what constitutes "awareness" allows for assigning all sorts of signals and cues to the category of unconscious. The question before us is one of better delineating the nature of the messages that go on between people. To assume that a particular emotional state experienced by one person is a response to unconscious signals rather than to subtle but recognizable signals is a conceptual leap that may be unwarranted.

Just as open to question is the assumption that the said state is a reaction of the analyst *to* a patient's communication rather than an initiating message *from* the analyst. The tendency is to insist on the innocence of the analyst. There is a need to clarify what is truly unconscious communication, if such exists, and what qualifies for awareness on the part of the analyst. There is a world of difference between not noticing, for a variety of reasons up to and including psychological defenses, and not being able to notice, which might properly belong to phenomena such as Bion's raw sense data. Sullivan's (1953) "selective inattention" is an outstanding illustration of the former type of not knowing.

One welcome clarification of messages that are transmitted but not acknowledged is the study of nonverbal communication, which is credited primarily to Wilhelm Reich (1933) but is now an object of contemporary study as well (Jacobs, 1994). Such an exchange is felt to be omnipresent but in need of deciphering, since the interactions are fleeting and need a trained observer. Jacobs (1994) cautions us that we develop or persist in having scotoma that cause us to miss a great deal of what is transmitted between patient and analyst. The position of the proponents of "unconscious communication," however, is that it is not possible to be aware of the transmission of raw sense data which is surely received but not registered as such, inasmuch as it is in need of some sort of transformation. So too is projective identification explained as a series of unconscious steps culminating in "an experience that is only able to be acknowledged at its culmination" (Goldstein, 1991).

One problem that arises here is that of defining better what we mean by saying that we are not conscious or aware of something that we later experience. Consciousness is said by some philosophers to be a "mongrel concept" (Block, 1995) and by psychologists to be a polysemous term with many meanings (Natsoulas, 1978). Psychoanalysts, following Freud, seem to focus mainly on a single meaning, that of paying attention to, as when the eye of consciousness focuses on some particular idea or event. Yet we know that many conscious events are regularly not attended to, although they are clearly not preconscious. Riding along on a crowded highway is an oft-used example of our consciously maneuvering our cars while we are able to attend to a conversation or listen to the news. Jacob's point of training persons to decipher nonverbal communication also seems to speak to a sort of consciousness that lies outside of immediate awareness (i.e., that which is phenomenal or experienced). Indeed, psychoanalysis has long entertained the concept of disavowal as referring to an arena of the mind that is accessible in the sense of its not being repressed and its being regularly kept from experience or conscious awareness. So, as a start, it is possible to think of much of this unrecognized communication as sets of signals received in the usual way but separated from one's immediate experience. Is this now, at a minimum, a reasonable alternative to theoretical concepts that involve transmission of information that functions on a quasi-mystical level from one unconscious to another, from alpha and beta elements to states of reverie, or from imaginary representations in one mind taking up residence in another?

The existence of some split-off material, which may at times be phenomenologically unconscious but clearly accessible to consciousness, makes its presence known in certain situations, especially those involving treatment. Its emergence in a therapeutic situation may take many forms, some of which will depend on the patient and some on the therapist. For example, patients whose vertical split has to do with behavior may, at times and with certain therapists, evoke a variety of behaviors in the therapist. Some of this may be, in turn, acknowledged by the therapist but some, not surprisingly, may be split off by the therapist herself. Thus, at times, there occurs a kind of mutual acting that is never brought into an arena of scrutiny or study but seems to exist and persist in a conspiracy of silence. Sometimes the split-off segment is talked about briefly but meets with such a condemning attitude by the therapist that it ceases to be mentioned yet continues to exist silently outside of the treatment in but a different form of conspiracy: one that allows the therapist to disavow a significant part of the patient's pathology and thereby maintain a personal comfort that is not in the best interests of the treatment.

All sorts of intermediary positions between the banished segment and the reciprocally acted-on segment seem to find a place in treatment. It is not immediately clear what exactly is the best method or technique to manage or effectively interpret these various positions, nor is it clear how these disavowed contents can be allowed to present themselves. For example, it is a tenet of analytic lore that, over time, unconscious repressed material will manage to emerge, perhaps in disguised form, in the treatment situation. Whether in dreams, symptoms, or transference, the derivatives of the unconscious gain a hearing. The repressed material achieves an outlet. No such certainty seems to obtain with disavowed material, which may succeed in remaining completely outside of the treatment situation. Some of this absence can be attributed to the naïve or opaque therapist, but some of it may also be due to a failure to allow it to enter openly into the treatment. It is not at all uncommon to hear from a patient that, as in one example, "Never during my long analysis did I mention to my analyst that I regularly stole books that I neither needed nor read, before, during, and after the treatment." Perhaps this analyst would be surprised and shocked to hear this, but we would be foolish to condemn the analyst for this supposed failure. It is a much more common occurrence than we may wish to believe.

To better understand the place of disavowal and the fate of the vertically split-off material, we need to understand its origin, development, and continued status in the psyche. To understand the management and treatment of these phenomena, we need to understand the reciprocal role of the same phenomena in the therapist. Together they seem to compose the field of discourse that includes all of the previously noted struggles with communications that seem nonverbal, unrecognized, or too quickly dismissed. Being of two minds does seem to require some sort of place or home for each of them. Sometimes this duality can be realized in treatment, and sometimes the disavowed part must find a place for itself elsewhere.

From the simple fact of ambivalence, it is a small step to the complex state of parallel but separate personalities, and so the concept of a vertical split presents itself. In a psychological encounter, there is no easy way to comprehend and communicate with another person who is forever concealing an aspect of himself. Originally in our theory that concealed aspect was felt to be inaccessible to the person, which gave rise to the concept of repression. But a common and equally troublesome separate self that is not repressed seems also to tax our efforts. We turn next to a study of that other form of separation and how it manifests itself.

Chapter 3

THE FAILURE OF SYNTHESIS: THE PHENOMENOLOGY OF THE VERTICAL SPLIT

We are all regularly invited to share in a "willing suspension of disbelief" (Coleridge, 1817) when we are watching a movie or a play. As much as we know the production to be make-believe, we cannot enjoy the spectacle unless we leave behind or deny for a while the entirety of the reality that engaged us before the curtain rose. Aside from documentaries that may insist on involving our sense of reality, all of the fictional renditions demand that we temporarily abandon our grounding in the real world. No one would claim, however, that what has sometimes been termed a "regression in the service of the ego" is necessarily a state of opposition. It is clearly more in the sense of a unified and comfortable tolerance of a different state of mind. One may wonder, however, if the same state applies to the child who plays at being a powerful person but quickly heeds the parental call to brush his or her teeth. A bit of opposition may appear here. The child is momentarily living in two worlds or experiencing two realities. It is only in the origins and functions of the coexistence of differences that we will be able to clarify when one is forced to deny something (i.e., another reality) and when one is amused by it and can tolerate its coexistence. When Anna Freud (1936) discussed denial by phantasy, word, and act she was speaking of a defense against an unwelcome reality, a real opposition. The use of the word *denial*, however, has been extended to cover such a wide variety of psychological maneuvers that it is necessary for us to examine just how it develops and what is made of it before we can ascertain its place in pathology or normality. Some denial seems healthy and normal; some may qualify as pathological. The range of the split and some suggestions as to its origin will be the focus of this chapter.

Origins of Separation of States of Mind

One interesting approach to the problem of disavowal is examined by Bowlby (1980) in his chapter entitled "An Information Processing Approach to Defense." There Bowlby discusses the exclusion of information that is received and selectively kept outside of awareness for reasons of psychological adaptation. He discusses ideas of subliminal perception, where something is registered but not consciously experienced, and what he terms "perceptual defense," and he describes experiments wherein sensory information is not allowed full access to consciousness. Bowlby takes into consideration dissociative states such as hypnosis, problems of episodic and semantic memory, and various formulations of the self. In regard to the last, he poses the question of whether a person may have more than one self, and he suggests that an individual may have either a unified or an un-unified Principal System, a phrase that he introduces as relevant to the capacity for self-reflection. Bowlby discusses the role of "cognitive disconnection" in psychopathology, with an emphasis on loss and responses to loss. He emphasizes, however, that the propensity for defensive exclusions is derived from the early years from issues surrounding attachment behavior and can continue throughout a person's development. He does feel that defensive exclusion can be adaptive as well as maladaptive. There is a brief discussion of repression but no mention of Freud's work on disavowal. The significance of this work is its focus on observations that seem to qualify as examples of a vertical split in the very early formative years. He has less to say about how this division is experienced by the split person, and he never pursues or explains just how attachment difficulties lead to defensive exclusion.

Another approach to the disavowal discussion is offered by Penot (1998), who uses Freud's case of the Wolf Man to illustrate the rejection of reality in disavowal in keeping the meaning in suspension (i.e., in refraining from a judgment about a fact of the patient's history). In his discussion of Freud's use of terms to describe the rejection of reality, Penot notes that Lacan proposed the term "foreclosure" to designate "a rejection of a psychical representation out of the symbolic order," and he goes on to clarify that this suspension of judgment or inability to participate in symbolization is quite different from negation. Penot discusses issues similar to those that we shall deal with in the analyst's role in treating disavowal and nicely sums up his position by stating: "Disavowal is a narcissistic expedient by which the subject frantically tries to spare himself the experience of the absences and shortcomings of his parental figures (in compliance with the parents' own narcissistic defense)" (p. 35).

Bonnie Litowitz (1998) has suggested a developmental line for denial, a word that, like disavowal, has over time unfortunately become a wastebasket for the process of ridding ourselves of unpleasantness, whether in the form of a momentary experience or in the existence of an ongoing state of affairs, that is, one that we are incapable of reckoning with. Litowitz posits the sequence of rejection, refusal, and denial as she notes the developing child's capacity to deal with the varied expressions and behavior of negation. Litowitz also notes that all of the members of this sequence remain operative. Heretofore the recognition of the sequential occurrence of psychological phenomena has routinely led psychoanalysis to characterize the persistence or reappearance of early behavior as reflective of a fixation at that time of first appearance or as indicative of a pathology based on the state of development at that particular time. That characterization seems no longer to be valid. We seem able to employ different states of denial at different times.

To recall what Gedo and I previously wrote: "Earlier functional capacities always persist, both in their original 'primitive' forms and in the various progressively more 'mature' forms they may attain. Development proceeds by the progressive addition of new structures which operate in parallel with earlier ones and which permit the maturation of the latter" (Gedo and Goldberg, 1973, p. 156). It may well be the case that even this statement now needs both qualification and reemphasis. Perhaps it is more appropriate to say that there is no real persistence of earlier forms. Rather, the developing psyche uses whatever is needed. Indeed, the entire concept of developmental lines may now be open to challenge. There is no doubt that, as Litowitz shows, behavior does indeed appear in stages, but the image of a single and progressive line may be quite untenable. Susan Coates (1977) states that the concept of a developmental line has outlived its usefulness. Thelen and Smith (1994) in their presentation of a dynamic systems approach to development, along with Shane, Shane, and Gales (1997), have emphasized that development does not proceed along a line but rather in complex, nonlinear, and unpredictable forms. Efforts to delineate stages, phases, and hierarchies now seem obsolete and unwarranted. Thus we see that rejection, refusal, and denial may all participate in the formation of what is also termed sublation (Litowitz, 1998). That term was suggested first by the philosopher Hegel to refer to what is both abolished and yet preserved, to what is canceled but essentially saved and put to the side. It is an element that is never completely synthesized but rather remains in the dialectic, in the ongoing to-and-fro. Litowitz (1998) sees sublation in dialectics of good and bad, subjective and objective, losing and keeping. It seems ideally suited to describe what occurs in both our patients and ourselves when we seem regularly to embrace and discard a part of the self. Thus the experience of splitting can be seen to span across one's life both in frequency and in intensity. It is a psychical operation that is available to some all their lives and to others at particularly crucial times (Freud, 1940).

Imagine the mind of the university professor who is regarded as a scholar of intellectual and moral integrity. Periodically, he finds it necessary to enter one or another bookstore in his college town and, after scanning the shelves, steal several books which he conceals within his coat. These are, routinely, books that he has no particular use for and certainly has no plans ever to read. Indeed the books' fate after the theft is of little moment, and they may well be discarded. The excitement and urgency of the theft, however, override all considerations of need and necessity. Once stolen they have lost their value and purpose. But also, once stolen, they carry a message of shame for our teacher, who feels terrible about what he has done and who pledges never to repeat this kind of behavior, which is totally out of keeping with the way he sees himself. He thereby rejects that thieving part of himself but, also, in the characteristic meaning of sublation, he retains the behavior as well. No matter how firmly he insists that he must disown the thief, he has simultaneously preserved him in another place, for another time, as the need arises.

The mind of the person who denies an unwelcome bit of reality, such as in mourning the loss of a loved one, the mind of the spectator at a play who suspends her disbelief to enjoy the performance, and the mind of the child who plays with the forces of good and evil all bear a resemblance to our thief but are nowhere near so torn in two. They all indulge in play or fantasy and then return to a different reality—perhaps with regret rather than with shame. Our thief goes beyond fantasy to action. Not all of our occasional thieves feel much shame, however, so the presence of shame is not an absolute guide to the difference between the split of the ordinary person versus that of the misbehaving person. The initial important point is that the disowned behavior of the truly split is both scorned and saved, but never discarded despite one's resolve. It is retained in another place and returned to periodically. It thereupon becomes a refuge and an indulgence and remains available as the need arises. It is to the fundamentals of the need that we must now look to for a better explanation of its origin.

The Function of Disavowal

Litowitz (1998) claims that the earliest forms of negation—rejection and refusal—appear in the first year of life, and here she concurs with Bowlby. She notes that Spitz (1957) feels that rejection involves a response to the environment but not to persons. Refusal, the phase that developmentally follows rejection, has to do with the response to what is asked of the person by another; it is part and parcel of communication. Denial is seen as the negation of another person's statement and is the clearest form of an interpersonal issue. In a sense, these three stages of negation all participate in the disavowal that we see in our patients; the sequence inevitably becomes an organized effort and often becomes a necessary part of the psyche. We can start to see how it operates in a communicative network along with a personal adaptive sense. The following case study shows its function in a patient.

Carol, the patient (chapter 1) with an eating disorder, describes a childhood of intense difficulty with an anxious and intrusive mother. Carol thought of her early life in two phases: one of a happy comfort lying on her couch and reading, and another of bitter arguments with her mother. These arguments seemed to center in the kitchen and were struggles over control. Interestingly, her reading was accomplished primarily within earshot of her mother. She liked to feel that Mother was around, but she did not wish to engage with her in what were inevitably either arguments or exasperating discussions. Thus, with this proximity, Carol seemed to avoid the loss and depression that later surfaced in her adult life and led her to treatment. When she began her "other" life of bingeing, it was a successful effort in her attempt to avoid that incipient and haunting depression, and it was then that the denial or disavowal in the form of the emergence of a parallel or other person became evident. But that other person was herself. It was Carol engaged once again in a struggle over control and managing thereby to reactivate a childhood situation, bring her mother and the childhood situation back, and obliterate her sadness. She thereby manages to avoid her depression. In the bingeing she refuses to submit to her mother, while she effectively denies the part of herself that insists on the experience of that depression. She is momentarily emancipated but out of contact. After the eating spree, she proceeds to deny that other part of herself that has lost control. That last denial is also a saving or suspension, inasmuch as she has managed to retain the binge eater in order for her to be available wherever and whenever the potential upset of loss and depression rears its head. This onset of one or another particular form of behavior or misbehavior is routinely signaled by some form of intense and unbearable feeling, a feeling that is relieved by one or another form of behavior. Carol has a part or segment of herself that is subject to depression when she is left alone along with a parallel part that overeats and rids her of the depression. Neither part is able to happily live with the other, but each does seem to tolerate the other. Her behavior both tells us something about her split and effectively allows her to forestall her depression.

Lothstein (1997) describes a cross-dresser who "transformed himself from a depressed, lonely, and panicky individual into an 'ecstatic' individual who felt alive, excited and beautiful." Prior to cross-dressing, he experienced a "dreamy state" (p. 108).

Lothstein's thesis also involves a bridge or connection to an absent mother. The disavowal per se does not ensue unless and until there is a negative reaction to the behavior, as a result of which the person in question is compelled to split off his misbehaving (i.e., cross-dressing) self from his self that behaves more acceptably in front of others. This setting apart or separation of that person who engages in a behavior such as cross-dressing, which is felt to be undesirable from the standpoint of the more proper and acceptable person, is needed to be used in the management of painful affective states, which are short-circuited and are never allowed to be fully experienced. The solution insists that an available but unacknowledged person is allowed to pursue an activity that solves a problem. This "misbehaving" other person, however, does not ever become a true member of the psychological household. The varied attitudes that develop toward this "other self" help to explain further the failure at synthesis that characterizes this pathology. This supposed failure can now be seen as an effort to avoid the pain that integration would bring. But now we see the price that must be paid for retaining the split inasmuch as the failed synthesis both saps the energy that would be available to an integrated person and demands an accounting for living in a real world.

The Two Realities

Some philosophers (Goodman, 1978) like to tell us that we all live in different worlds with different perceptions and attitudes, and ultimately with our own personal knowledge about the world. Others claim that there is surely but one single world we all inhabit no matter how and what we make of it. For the first, reality is very much the world that we create. For the second, reality is immune to how we choose to fashion it; rather, the world is an immutable given that allows all sorts of interpretations, but these are all essentially renditions rather than other realities. Thus, one says that rocks are rocks no matter what we may say or think about them; the other says that there are no rocks until we decide to agree that there are. If we follow the idea of a single reality, we are committed to ideas about what is true and correct, especially as regards an accurate portrayal of the world. If we follow the second view, we allow for relative considerations of truth and facts that become based on individual estimations and perceptions. One man's pleasure is not the same as another's, and one man's morality differs as well from another's.

Freud (1927), in his discussion of fetishism, very clearly indicated that the little boy had both a right way and a wrong way of seeing the world. In terms of reality, the boy correctly saw that the little girl had no penis. In terms of fantasy, he imagined and hoped that the little girl did possess a penis. Thus Freud posited a split between what came to be called the reality ego (i.e., the correct and true vision of the world) and the split-off unreal sector (i.e., the one that allowed a wished-for but false state of affairs to exist). If we step back from the immediacy of the actual presence of the penis, however, we may allow for a more metaphoric sense of the girl's penis as a condition that signifies power or strength and not as a claim wholly attributable to a specific configuration of a genital organ. This view then allows license for a reconsideration of the split-off sector as claiming not an unreal or fantasized set of facts as much as an acceptance of a different take on reality, one that corresponds to a different collection of facts and perceptions. Along with the embracing of this other system of reality, one brings a corresponding set of moral evaluations and judgments that pertain to such issues as goals, ideals, and aims; these issues in turn determine which reality will lay claim to the behavior of the individual at any given time and place. Thus, reality becomes more than perception in any pure sense of registration; it encompasses a host of accompanying psychological needs and wishes. Having two minds asks the person to see the world as different at different times just as Freud's little boy saw the girl as both having and lacking a penis.

There is little doubt that the maintenance of differing or separate realities is often both tolerable and welcome. They are tolerable if there exists little or no clash between, say, the value systems of each, and they are welcome if the adoption of one is more liable to lead to feelings of pleasure and comfort. It is also apparent that such differing realities can become a source of discomfort and worry if the pleasure aims and value systems are at odds with one another. Indeed, it is routine that sooner or later one reality or mind-set adopts an attitude of critical evaluation and assessment toward the other. It is here that we begin to see the life of disavowal wherein each mind or self needs to banish the other rather than continue a conscious life of coexistence. We begin to see statements such as "I do not like myself when. . . ." And so the person is split in two.

We would do well to remember that the so-called break with reality said to be true of psychotic individuals is likewise an adoption of a different reality. It was about this point that Freud insisted that there was always a separate part of the most delusional person that remained in touch with what he claimed was "reality" (Breuer and Freud, 1893–1895). Freud preferred to speak of this latter domain as objective reality in opposition to a psychic reality. Others often speak of the patient's reality versus the analyst's reality. It is not always clear whether psychic reality is necessarily unconscious as Freud insisted it was, or whether it has conscious components as others have claimed (Rosenblatt, 1997). Perhaps this is best explained by recognizing that each segment of the severed self seems to participate in both an objective and a psychic reality, that is, one that perceives the world in a certain way *and* has unconscious motives and components. No matter how we deal with these terms, we need to retain the image of a person who lives at one time or another in two separated worlds or is of two minds, one of which may have a stronger claim to the reality of others. It often becomes an intolerable state of affairs, and this is sometimes first reckoned with in treatment.

In his consideration of psychic reality, Freud (1900, p. 613) said that the unconscious was the true psychic reality, but in his discussion of disavowal he was obliged to concede that this latter defense was turned against *external* reality; repression was not an issue. To bring the analyst's versions of objective and psychic reality to bear requires more than a simple negotiation and discussion of how each of the participants sees, feels, and understands the world. *That* debate is well handled by Rosenblatt, who claims that the open recognition and use of one's reality is a valuable albeit fallible guide (Rosenblatt, 1997, p. 405). The situation is made complex because the analyst must somehow respond to the dual version of the world by a (often unrecognized) duality of his or her own. A patient who reports some behavior to you that you and he both find undesirable and repugnant makes a clear claim of being torn about what he finds both necessary and awful. These two states may occasionally appear close in time. This patient asks of the analyst a corresponding meeting to and with each of these states. And indeed the patient may feel differently about each of them: that is his subjective reality. But the states may as well clearly have a recognizably acceptable status in the community that is their objective reality. And they likewise derive from some unconscious material that is unrelated one state to the other, which is their psychic reality. Things get complicated. Some people do live in two worlds as they think and feel differently about each of them. They may say they are different persons or the same person with two ways of living that cannot tolerate one another.

Rosenblatt (1997) prefers not to tackle the philosophical question of whether there is but one objective verifiable reality rather than a multiplicity of equally valid realities (p. 398). At least one philosopher, however, (Searle, 1995), helps us out by clarifying the difference between "objective facts" and "social facts." The first has to do with what is "intrinsic" whereas the second is said to be "observer relative." Whether the moon causes tides is objective. Whether the moon is beautiful is a matter of judgment. To return to our book thief, there is no doubt that he can be objective about the facts related to stealing, but he may feel differently than you and I would when he is engaged in stealing. He has a vivid consensual objectivity about the state of affairs out there. It is in the matter of personal or subjective states of pleasure and moral values that a departure from that stance is evident. Only then and at that point does his reality differ from what may be the norms of society. The theft of the books is accomplished by a person who is intent on the achievement of a certain set of feelings, a pleasurable affective state that will undo or obliterate a nascently undesirable affective state. Thus the pleasure aim of the activity is a clear one. So, too, are the morals and values of our thief at variance with those of most societies, and those of the other part of the mind of the thief, which might, at another time, lay a different claim to virtue. But, during the theft, there is little doubt that stealing is the right and correct thing to do. Because the theft is both feasible and allowable in this particular psychic state, it becomes organized into a behavior that conforms to a focused vision of reality. Sooner or later, however, the triad of rejection, refusal, and denial of this other life comes into play as the university professor begins to look at what he has done. He reports in retrospect that he is aghast and disgusted at his behavior, which he utterly and completely disowns. "I regret it. I want nothing to do with it. It is as if it were an act of someone else. I shall never again do it." This then is the construction of the vertical split which treats that severed sector as offensive and thereupon disowned. The component that is yet to be added to complete the act involves reserving a place for this segment so that it can be revived and used as the need arises.

One must distinguish this thief and this misbehavior from the host of similar actions committed by those who have little or none of the thief's subsequent feelings of opposition and disgust. There can be little doubt that one must look very carefully for what Freud claimed was present in the most delusional of psychotics: the segment tied to objective reality. And even if this is discovered in place, in fact it is not, for many, a sector that seems to matter very much in an ongoing subjective reality. Most of these, let us say, essential thieves clearly know what is right but do not much care. They do not seem to live in a state of disavowal and discomfort very often, if at all. Perhaps, with some, this capability can be rehabilitated, as it is surely the single most significant point in any effort to diminish or eliminate the misbehavior. The one segment looking at and evaluating the other becomes the sine qua non of effective and meaningful intervention, an intervention that aims at some form of synthesis of the attitudes and forces that remain opposed and unyielding. With this explication of the failed synthesis, we can next turn to an examination of some of the contents of the separated parts.

Origins of Pleasure Aims and Valued Goals

Most children seem to grow and develop a consistent set of principles that direct them to feelings of pleasurable fulfillment and satisfaction. There is no need to repeat here the familiar story of the child's internalization by way of identification of the rules and regulations of what is considered by the parents to be proper behavior. Children who rebel against parental values are characterized as misbehaving; children who are overly fastidious about properness are noted to be exhibiting another form of psychopathology. Children who seem to fit in with parental and social mores are routinely seen as well adjusted. Within this set of social and individual constraints, there exists a range of acceptable pleasurable outlets that allow for a major set of motivations for proper behavior in the pursuit of gratification and enjoyment.

It would be a welcome note to say that cases of behavior disorders derive from one or more particular sets of circumstances
such as a configuration of family dynamics or even a targeted
genetic marker. A recent issue of the *Psychiatric News* (1997), for
example, announced that "childhood neglect" was a risk factor
for borderline disorders while simultaneously warning us that this
was not the "whole story." We have learned from recent concepts
in development that there is no "whole story," inasmuch as development is essentially haphazard and unpredictable. We do, however, seem to find certain common factors that exist in the
childhood of patients with behavior disorders, while recognizing
that these should not be thought of as necessarily a full explanation. They may be necessary but not sufficient conditions. More
is needed.

Lothstein (1997) reports a rather typical case of Jacob, a seven-
year-old boy who wore his mother's pantyhose whenever Mother
left the house. He is said to have experienced her leaving as "trau-
matogenic" and to have discovered that when he put on Mother's
stockings the fear, anxiety, and diffuse sense of panic left him. The
stockings bound his body. They were tight fitting and enclosed
him in a safe space. The top panel covered his penis, and when
Jacob looked in the mirror, he could not see his penis and felt
comforted. Lothstein reports that this boy fantasized himself as a
girl and would tuck his penis between his legs and pretend to
have a vagina. The pantyhose served to disguise his penis, and its
opaque panel acted as a shield. A series of these cases of
Lothstein's exhibit the persistence of this or similar types of such
behavior into adulthood. They are often regularly described as
beginning in childhood either by some accidental discovery of the
child, as with Jacob, or by some act of induction by a relative—
especially in those cases involving cross-dressing. What is routinely associated with the origins of these behaviors is the
acknowledgment or implicit acceptance of the behavior by one or
another parent. Thus, another case of Lothstein describes a
mother who felt that her four-year-old wearing her clothing was
"cute" and in fact became the basis for a favorite family story.
But just as one regularly sees tolerance for and acceptance of the
behavior, one sees as well the opposite message of condemnation
and disdain. The same mother who thinks it cute brings the boy
for a psychiatric consultation a few years later when the boy
denies wearing her clothes. The boy has now achieved the verti-

cal split with the aid of a similarly segmented parent. We shall presently posit that a reciprocal split lives in the mother who both promotes and dislikes her child's behavior.

One must exercise caution in assigning the essential cause of the split seen in behavior of this type to the malignant influence of a parent, usually the mother. The particular influence of the (say) mother is often complex and subtle and will be discussed at length in the next chapter. Nonetheless, the compliance and tolerance of a mother frequently play a key role or are frequently implicated in the production and maintenance of a division in a child. Here are two examples. The first, mentioned in a previous publication (Goldberg, 1995), is of a mother who before marriage had given birth to a baby girl. The baby was immediately placed for adoption. When the patient, a male, was born to his now married mother, it seemed clear that she longed for and indeed actively searched for her lost little girl. The patient's father was not the father of this baby girl, but seemed to join with his wife in wanting a little girl. The patient took to wearing girl's clothes at an early age and delighted in masturbating in front of a mirror while presenting himself as a female. This mother seemed clearly to communicate to her son that she wished him to be a girl, but also recognized that he was a boy. Our cross-dressing patient was thereby both boy and girl, both real and unreal, or experiencing different realities. The multitude of other factors that participate in the onset and continuation of cross-dressing, however, do not allow for too simple a conclusion about its cause.

Another mother would threaten her little boy with placing him in diapers long after he was toilet trained, whenever he would seem to manifest any sort of babyishness or neediness. He developed a fantasy of being diapered, and thereafter he found a network of such people on the Internet, all of whom became sexually aroused and masturbated with this very particular fantasy. What became clear in his treatment was that his neediness and dependency had simply been too much for this overworked mother. Her communication to the child ultimately directed him to find one or another behavioral outlets that would handle these needs, albeit in an aberrant manner. That is, the mother fostered and supported any activity that absorbed the demandingness of the child and so relieved her. And just as the mother of the cross-dressing child insisted that the child's behavior was not to be condoned while subtly encouraging it, so there was a parallel acceptance of the diaper fantasy with masturbation by this second mother. Admittedly, many if not most of these mothers either claim ignorance of, or vehemently deny, any acceptance of these behaviors. But the mother is split just as the child. The split in the mother comes from either opposing perceptions of the child or alternating propensities of the mother to function adequately for the child. Thus the tense and anxious child who handles the separation from the mother by wearing pantyhose is helping to solve the mother's inability adequately to comfort the child by his development of this symptomatic behavior. This solution is subsequently accepted and condemned. Each would claim a disavowal of its acceptance. So, too, the boy who has to be both male and female is responding accurately to a mother who would clearly deny that unspoken request of the child. Mother and child each live in two worlds and embrace two realities. Later I show how this match of a split parent and a split child is reenacted in an analytic treatment.

To be sure, there is a meeting and a match between parent and child in the construction and maintenance of a split in one's life. The contribution of the parent, however, does not take the form of a clear communication, and a variety of factors contribute to the particular form and content of the split and the ensuing behavior. Patients with eating disorders may or may not report a childhood of handling anxiety through bingeing, and exhibitionists rarely tell of parents who openly supported that manner of deviance. The fundamental feature resides less in the manifested behavior and more in the parents' inability to form and maintain an integrated image of the child. The failure of such an integration will only lead to lifelong difficulties if the two segments are fundamentally at odds with each other. The male versus the female, the needy versus the independent, the shy versus the forthright are all forerunners of a necessary division that cannot be comfortably synthesized into a unit but rather must remain apart and at odds. What follows is some consideration of just how they are kept apart.

Turning a Blind Eye

It is safe to say that the childhood of individuals who behave in one or another manner they find distasteful yet necessary was constructed jointly with one or both parents. It would not be fair to say, however, that this formation of a split was actively or openly encouraged or condoned by the parent who would correctly and honestly claim either ignorance or innocence. The nature of the support and tolerance of behavior that would seem to be clearly at odds with the moral code and principles of the parent is best explained by our recognition of the parent's inability to be aware of its existence along with the qualification that this particular term, "awareness," needs to be better examined.

Recent work on the capacity of certain individuals who fail to comprehend the nonverbal cues of others (Palombo, 1997) demonstrates that these same individuals also have a defect in their own capacity to communicate nonverbally. Palombo notes that we convey messages about our feelings and read others' messages of how they feel about us by way of gaze, vocal intonation, gesture, and interpersonal proximity. If these messages are encoded but disavowed, they may become later enacted in the form of a nonverbal recall. This might explain some of the episodic disavowed behavior, but perhaps we can move to any earlier point in an effort to begin to explain the disavowal per se.

The spectrum of caregivers who are unable to read the needs and feelings of a child correctly range from the depressed mother who cannot free herself from her unhappiness long enough to be in touch with her child, to the learning-disabled mother who cannot comprehend the child whose needs are communicated outside the verbal sphere. Further, there is the learning-disabled child who is unable adequately or effectively to communicate his or her needs to the care givers. Recognizing that there is no such thing as perfect empathy, one realizes that there is a range of parents who are relatively attentive and responsive to their children, and a range of children able to make their wishes and feelings known. There is a complex interchange in this communicative exchange. We often say that the child's deidealization of the parent occurs with the first successful lie, but surely the parent who cannot read the child's needs invites a very early and possibly traumatic state of deidealization. On one hand, this child may develop a conviction that he or she can get away with things, that one can operate in a world without parental intervention or know-how, that parents are less than perfect. On the other hand, the child may need to sacrifice a great deal of autonomy to maintain what is essentially a vital selfobject tie.

Thus the child feels trapped between living up to the standards of the parent and exercising another outlet to maintain some psychological equilibrium. Somehow, somewhere, he or she learns what the parents will allow to ease everyone's discomfort.

Inasmuch as every child proceeds through the stages of deidealization, of coming to see the parent as human and fallible, we need to ask what other factors may be operative in and around the parental failure to heed the message of the child. Lothstein's (1997) cases are representative, inasmuch as all of these patients characterize their childhood experience *before* the onset of their cross-dressing as one of intense anxiety and near panic. Most of the descriptive literature on sexual perversions seems to suggest a specific dynamic constellation to the behavior or else posits a chance discovery of behavior that relieves the anxiety and panic as noted in the wearing of pantyhose. Whatever the origin, the parent is unable to see the fear of the child both because of his or her own limitations and because of the fact that the unhappy child is no longer around. The child has disappeared, has found a solution. He or she has discovered a split-off way of relieving the anxiety, and this is somehow registered and appreciated by the parent who implicitly prefers a misbehavior that can be ignored to a depression that cannot be.

These parental failures to meet the needs of the child often become coupled with the child's failure to communicate his needs. The nonverbal learning-disabled child is always thrown back on his own resources as he finds the world to be disorganized and unresponsive. Having to find oneself as well as soothe and regulate oneself is an appeal to one's grandiosity and one's personal need to control all of the facets of the world. It seems an easy step to construct such a separate world—without interference—one that is totally at the demand of the moment. That we see this possibility in a learning-disabled child should not lead us to feel that all such children and adults are neurologically impaired. The more obvious communicative failure seen in these patients can be extrapolated to similar problems in other parents who are unresponsive because of a range of conditions such as depression or substance abuse. Basch (1988) claimed that disavowal is fostered by an environment in childhood with parents who did not encourage, and often positively discouraged, discussion of anxiety-provoking issues (p. 126). The child feels that not talking or thinking about painful events allows one to escape their emotional consequences. Because Basch felt that disavowal entailed a disconnection between the perception of an experience and the affect it evoked, he likened its occurrence to a neurological disconnection between the hemispheres of the brain. It is an interesting possibility, because the learning-disabled patient seems to offer a potential clinical experiment. At a minimum there seems to be a similarity in the basic issue of the parent not being able to respond fully to certain sets of distress signals from the child. This phenomenon, then, comprises the special sort of blindness that characterizes the interaction.

9/24/02

Recapitulation

From the disagreeable to the alien, from the distasteful to the unbearable, disavowal allows a separation in the psyche that may be maintained and then used as the occasion demands. The overcoming of this separation calls for a bringing together, a synthesis of the irreconcilable, and an achievement of integration. The maintenance of the split allows for a somewhat happy compromise of what seems to be an unholy alliance. Because the activity of disavowal is universal, its categorization as pathological or helpful depends on its utility along with its moral standing.

The initial step or stage in the formation of the disavowed or vertical split is regularly reconstructed as some negative affective experience of the child. Our patient with an eating disorder seemed to struggle with depression; others may experience anxiety bordering on panic or disintegration. There seems to be a rather tight coupling of this negative affect with the emotional unavailability of the caregiver. The particular psychological functions of the parent who becomes absent will be explored and explained, but this absence seems to be the spur that initiates the discomfort and mobilizes the method to manage it. The crucial consideration here, which will require elaboration, is the capacity of the child to endure the experience of the particular distress. All sorts of factors come to bear here, because much depends on the intensity of the negative affect and the likelihood of immediate relief or assistance. If it is unbearable or intolerable, two psychic maneuvers may ensue. One is disavowal; the other is an activity that brings relief.

This construction of a split-off sector that is involved in some form of misbehavior becomes the hallmark of a separation that involves some new form of pleasure or relief along with a changing set of goals and values. The patient with an eating disorder finds the action or behavior to be relieving and pleasurable, but primarily she manages to obliterate her depression. Accompanying this behavior is an altered value having to do with body image and appearance. The patient who regularly employed prostitutes erased his anxiety while he gained pleasure in the sexual performance. He also needed to make a rather drastic realignment of his personal values, however, to be both unfaithful and dishonest. Each of these patients probably had some modicum of parental acceptance of these alternative pursuits. Numerous possibilities can be entertained from the accidental discovery by the child of some relieving behavior, to the suggestion and encouragement of it by a parent. The parent may be so preoccupied and negligent that no notice of the behavior is taken, or else the parent may exercise his or her own form of disavowal up to and including phrases such as "he will grow out of it" or "I did something like that when I was younger" or "it doesn't seem so terrible to me." That it does, however, engender some negative or oppositional feeling is a needed factor in the split being maintained rather than the maladaptive behavior dominating the personality. We see the latter in cases of substance abuse, in which hardly a sliver of a protesting other self can be revived. The split-off segment can evolve into a temptation rather than a relief, in that it is capable of assuming an easily tolerable and rarely condemned position. Unfortunately, many observers of behavior disorders focus on the pleasurable component of the activity and neglect the origin and initial purpose of its presence. In truth, many people live with split-off behavior of unusual and problematic nature throughout their lives. If one can fashion a niche in life for these sporadic forays, they can earn a certain privileged place in appearance and acceptance. There are cases that either are never seen by mental health professionals or else are kept outside of any treatment processes. The categories that do come to the attention of professionals are those that grow in frequency over time to the point of becoming out of control, along with those that eventuate in problematic situations because of discovery, legal or otherwise. This is essentially a condition in which the separate reality ceases to be allowed any existence at all.

Two Case Illustrations

A high school teacher was referred to a psychiatrist for the treatment of depression. Rather than opting for antidepressant medication, the psychiatrist and patient decided on psychotherapy, because the patient seemed to talk easily and respond well. During the course of telling about his life, the teacher disclosed a secret and separate life wherein he invited teenage boys to a hotel room and asked them to talk to him about their life. The teacher remained fully clothed, as did the boys, and at no time did he as much as touch them. He merely listened. After a while, the boy would leave with a few dollars given to him for his time and services. The patient would then masturbate with the mere memory of the encounter. He reported these episodes to his psychiatrist with a great deal of shame and with the assurance of his resolve not to repeat them. These reports were usually accompanied by a diatribe against many of his fellow teachers who, he claimed, were guilty of much more sinful sexual behavior. But the teacher also made it clear to his therapist that he had no wish to have this periodic behavior become an arena of psychological inquiry. Although the behavior was clearly pathological, the patient did not seem to want a solution. Indeed, as his depression lifted, he decided rather quickly to terminate his treatment with only the most positive of feelings toward the therapy. Afterward, the therapist was unable to explain fully just where this split-off segment of this man's mind was involved in the depression inasmuch as it did not seem to belong to the major part of his life. There did not appear to be much of a question as to its being clearly pathological, but neither did it seem to be a problem wanting a solution. The therapist had little doubt that it would continue to play a part in this man's life.

This example of a patient with a vertical split demonstrates its lifelong persistence with no effort to have it relieved or modified by treatment. It seems likely that innumerable cases similar to this one, though perhaps less unusual, do exist, and patients continue to function in a manner that allows the split to be maintained. The degree of shame or guilt engendered by the behavior is often insufficient to warrant a therapeutic intervention, because the threat of removing this outlet opens the door to a greater threat of reexperiencing the painful states of anxiety and depression that were responsible for the initiation of the split. Because this man was able to tolerate and endure the routine self-chastisement that he experienced after one of these episodes, there was no impetus for change. Not surprisingly, he was able to avail himself of psychotherapeutic help for his depression by making it clear that his parallel self was not to be tampered with or disturbed. And indeed, his depression did diminish and disappear although his split continued to exist. Contrast this outcome with the following case vignette.

This young and successful lawyer decided to undergo an analysis because of his inability to get married despite a series of intense and even enjoyable relationships with women whom he considered to be desirable. In the course of his treatment, he told of a habitual and secret ritual consisting of masturbating while watching pornographic films. In actual fact, there was one such film that he watched regularly. He said that he had no great need for variety, inasmuch as he chose to focus on the woman's breasts with little regard for the rest of the film. As his analysis proceeded, the particular place that his ritual had in his entire psychic economy became clearer, and it began to be talked about in his treatment as part and parcel of his reluctance to get more involved and intimate with the woman of the moment in his real life. His struggle with genuine closeness to a woman was necessarily viewed against this split-off outlet with his pornography. Here was a case wherein the segment of different behavior could not help but be disturbed. There was no way that his involvement with an artificial sexual activity could not figure in the treatment of his overall problems.

The treatment of persons whose lives are lived in two places ultimately aims at some synthesis into a unity, into a single set of integrated pleasure aims, values, and goals. We say "ultimately" or "ideally" with the full recognition that a number of compromises may be settled on. The recognition of the origin, development, and continuing role played by the split-off segment causes one to be sober about any effective intervention. A true therapeutic endeavor must relive the problems associated with the beginnings of the failed integration and yet must recognize that the pleasure component associated with what is often aberrant behavior is a powerful part of the resistance.

The road from the onset of a split that accompanies a behavior disorder is both nonlinear and often surprising. One report of a longitudinal study of 131 newborn infants and their parents

(Massie and Szajnberg, 1997) focuses on the one individual who developed a sexual fetish. The study makes it clear that even in retrospect no prediction of such a symptom is possible at this stage of our knowledge. Despite all of the accumulated hypotheses about the possible contributions to this one person's symptom, hypotheses involving castration anxiety, body-image difficulties, strong paternal involvement, and so forth, the conclusion reached was that we are no more likely to see a behavior disorder than a simple neurosis, that is, prediction is impossible. The missing ingredient in this and in other studies, it would seem, concerns the mind of the parents, and thus far, our best access to that is the potential reactivation of that mind in the therapist. The coexistence of a vertical split in both parent and child is the most fundamental feature of disorders such as fetishism. And somewhere, as noted, it must have started on its way with a parental acquiescence, not a malevolent one, but one that was directed to a solution for two parties and that remained so, long after the departure of the one.

Chapter 4

COLLUSION AND ITS PLACE
IN THE VERTICAL SPLIT

We have noted the ever-present role of subtle or overt parental encouragement or license in the early development of disavowal. For the most part, this phenomenon is seen in cases that manifest a clear, conscious separation of one way of behaving from that of another, that is, in cases that are designated either as narcissistic personality disorders or narcissistic behavior disorders. There is a more ubiquitous, but perhaps less clear occurrence of the split, however, found in certain states of disavowal in which the existence of the parallel personality yields little comfort or pleasure. The individual who suffers from this form of split regularly becomes overwhelmed by a dysphoria more akin to familiar psychological misfortunes such as seen in anxiety and depression rather than a specific behavioral activity. Thus it is proposed that disavowal and the vertical split span a host of maladaptations, with their origins to be found in particular forms of parental pathology.

To suggest that there are other forms of the vertical split is not to diminish its essential prominence in cases of both personality and behavior disorders, but rather to see if it is possible to better pinpoint how it comes about. A closer scrutiny of the developmental issues may allow an entry point into some metapsychological explanations. This is of particular value in an attempt to distinguish why one person will develop a behavior disorder, another a personality disorder, and yet another will have no such overt difficulty. Thus the split will be seen and examined in someone who seemingly has no relief whatsoever from the appearance of the parallel configuration.

When the vertical split was first proposed, it was put forth to characterize certain narcissistic personality disorders that showed a side-by-side disparate personality (e.g., grandiosity) along with reserve or aloofness (Kohut, 1971). This characterization was then expanded to the behavior disorders that displayed disparate behavior or misbehavior as in the sexual perversions. These two presentations were characteristic of narcissistic pathology, and they showed a structural difference with a corresponding structural deficiency in one sector that was seen as the pathological one, in contrast with a better structured, more realistic one. The present aim focuses on the developmental antecedents of the split and then tries to determine how it may be seen as pathological or adaptive. Here is one such illustration.

Case Illustration

Fritz M came to see a psychiatrist when he was in his early 50s after having been unsuccessful in several earlier attempts to ease his states of severe anxiety. These episodes occurred seemingly "out of the blue," in that they were unpredictable and were regularly related to worries and fears about his daughters and their safety, and he wondered if there was any psychopharmacologic medication that could help prevent these sudden and quite unforeseen attacks. The problem about his taking any medication was that the attacks were clearly connected to a specific worry about his children, and so he could live in relative comfort for long periods of time as long as he knew exactly where his girls were and just what they were doing. Under these circumstances he would feel relatively comfortable and thus quite foolish in his being medicated for a possible event that might not come about. He had read about panic attacks, but he felt that he did not clearly qualify for this disorder, inasmuch as he could always make the connection to a real and relevant worry that he had. To add to his uncertainty about what would be best for him was the fact that sometimes a supposed real and substantial cause for worry would pass with little notice and with little or no anxiety; at other times he could trace his experience and the related cause for worry only in retrospect. In all of those myriad ways he felt these unpleasant episodes as alien yet quite capable of over-whelming him. He tried and usually succeeded in hiding his anxious states from his family, but over the years everyone in the family knew that one had to reassure Fritz as to exactly where the girls were at any given moment. Thus he had formed a network of support without lessening the problem per se. His life, in a subtle way, became restricted, much like that of someone with a circumscribed phobia.

One interesting variation on his intense apprehension as to the safety and whereabouts of his daughters was primarily geographical. This was due to the fact that he drew an imaginary line of concern and control and, when they were far enough away, he seemed almost oblivious to what they might be doing. When asked, he immediately explained this by saying that there was nothing that he could do if they were overseas or in a faraway state, but that explanation flew in the face of that same fact of impotence being the case on numerous other occasions when they, for instance, were late in returning home at night. These latter times elicited more than the usual agitation of a frantic parent, because this patient seemed paralyzed with anxiety at a particular point that he had predetermined was the time for the return of his absent child. It was almost as if he became transformed from calm to terror at some magic moment involving an avalanche of fearful thoughts about one of his children, and this transformation was something that he despised. At first blush this may seem quite in keeping with an overly anxious parent, but Fritz felt that he was almost literally two persons: one in the grip of terror and the other with a realistic appraisal of the situation.

Fritz had gone to see a psychiatrist earlier in his life, before the issue of medication became relevant, but that venture had not been a success. He described that experience as a simple case of his becoming convinced that this particular professional was obviously unable to help, as well-meaning as he may have been. Fritz stayed with this psychiatrist long after this problem became evident to him, and he now looked back on this treatment as essentially a waste of time. Interestingly, he had much the same feeling toward many individuals in many walks of life, believing that no one was really capable of doing very much. This became known as "the emperor has no clothes" syndrome for this patient. He had little faith in the capacity of others to accomplish very much, and he never felt totally comfortable with the expectation that anyone would be able to accomplish anything, especially in the area of mental hygiene.

Fritz was born in Germany shortly before the Nazis came to power. His parents were Jewish, and his father worked as an academic in a university in a fairly large metropolitan city. The family, which consisted of Fritz and his older brother along with his parents, was described by him as middle-class and comfortable. The mother was a typical German hausfrau. They lived on the outskirts of this large city in a suburb that contained a number of other Jewish families. Their comfort included some few non-Jewish hired workers who cared for the children as well as cooked and cleaned house. Fritz commented on the fact that even after the rise of anti-Semitism in Germany, they continued to employ and be fond of these few house servants. But the major feature of his youth in Germany was Hitler's rise to power and the profound effect this had on his life and that of his family. There seemed to be a major and drastic disjunction as they changed from a family in relative ease and comfort to one in distress and unhappiness.

Going to school became one striking example of the change in Fritz's early life, because he quickly became aware of the fact that his teachers were openly anti-Semitic, and soon a few of his classmates began to tease and taunt him. This then developed into open physical assaults. Thus, when he was in early grade school, Fritz became a frightened and tormented boy. He could no longer walk down the street without a fear of being assaulted.

Along with this predicament was the recognition that his parents behaved as if nothing were wrong, that their lives were essentially unchanged, and that none of this trouble applied to them. Fritz thereupon never spoke of his fears or complained to his parents about what was happening to him. His older brother did, however, and he elicited no discernible response from Mother or Father. Fritz now smilingly says that they denied everything that was going on around them. He goes on to say that they continued to do so, despite the obviously worsening state of affairs that surrounded them. The virulence of the anti-Semitism increased. The misery attendant on the young boys going to school intensified. But the parents remained or behaved as though they were oblivious to it all. Some peculiar manner of regular but nonspoken communication seemed to be set up between his parents, primarily his father, and himself, so that Fritz was able to recognize and respond to the fact that he was never to talk about what was happening. Accompanying this more obvious recognition was another less obvious one: that his father was totally incapable of dealing with what was happening in their lives and country. This inability not only had to do with a clear lack of knowing what to do, but it also extended to a parallel one of not being capable of even acknowledging it at all.

Fritz reacted to his father's impotence with resignation. It did not seem to be something that one could argue over or fight against, as was the case with Fritz's brother, because it was not really a thing as much as it was a void. For Fritz, the message was clear: "There is nothing that can be done or should be done, and so there is nothing to talk about." And soon it came about that indeed there was nothing. And that qualifies as the start of the disavowal.

One can try to reconstruct just how Fritz managed simultaneously to know and not to know. He himself, of course, knew all about the growing antagonism to Jews, and he knew only too well that he was the target of this awful hatred. Yet he went regularly to school, and he behaved as if there were no change to his life. In this regard, he behaved exactly as his father would have him do. He thus seemed to heed and obey the messages from his father, messages that were never spoken and might even be denied if so spoken. What he did know was that it was necessary for his father to maintain a dualism of his own to survive. The son matched the father, while he simultaneously lived by himself in a totally different place. He did, however, pick up the cues that the father sent, in what he felt and saw, and how he expected Fritz to behave. On one hand, the messages of conformity to a nonexistent status quo were nonverbal as well as verbal, because Fritz knew these as a matter of course. They were clear if not loud. On the other hand, cues of fearfulness about the world were totally nonverbal but also quite clear, because father would not be able to hide his own fearfulness, and Fritz somehow saw that as well in his father. But although the accompanying messages were also nonverbal, they were admonitions not to speak. The only way to divide and separate out a mute, frightened boy from a brave, calm one was to create the side-by-side existence of the two.

The false unreal life of Fritz's family came to an end with the father's being summoned to Gestapo headquarters and summarily sent to a concentration camp. Released after several months, he returned to gather up his family and attempt to emigrate to America. Fritz, however, was sent beforehand to England and was reunited with his family after a year of living in a foster home with his brother and his new set of stand-in parents. Fritz dates the onset of episodes of anxiety to that period in England, but it became a regular member of his psychic household with the later birth of his own children. He recalls without hesitation the experience of acute anxiety as being a replica of what he experienced as he waited for his father outside Gestapo headquarters. The two had gone there together, but Fritz was not allowed in, and so he took up a position across the street to wait in abject terror for his father to emerge. Time passed, the father did not appear, and the stricken little boy found his way home alone. He says that this feeling is exactly what overwhelms him as he learns, for example, that one of his daughters is late in returning from some place or event. His panic sets in, and absolutely nothing relieves it until and unless she is safely back home. He regards this as a weakness and is manifestly ashamed of it but is powerless to forestall or prevent it. It is, of course, relieved immediately with the news of her arrival, but the advent of relief only makes him feel stupid and more ashamed of his disability.

This act of putting aside and then bringing back a totally foreign experience seems to exist in Fritz much the same as it does in our aforementioned thief, but other than the attendant shame after its termination, there is little else to join the two. It may be well at this point to suggest some of the possible dynamics and even outline a workable model to illustrate the problem. As a preamble, a brief overview of the psychoanalytic self-psychological ordering of the data is offered.

Joseph Sandler, in an article entitled "The Background of Safety" (1960) noted that "a feeling of safety develops from an integral part of narcissistic experience." He touched only briefly on its developmental origins but this was subsequently picked up by Heinz Kohut (1971) in his discussion of the path of development of idealization and the idealized parent. The latter is seen by the child as omnipotent and omniscient, as the child attempts to merge with that parental source of strength and control. Once the child is soundly connected to the greatness of the parent, who looks after, guides, and comforts the child, the resulting feeling is one of safety and protection. All children, it is posited, need to feel some form of protective presence to handle the discomforts and hurts of the world, and initially this is seen as residing in the parent who can dispel all difficulty and alleviate all misfortunes. This state would seem to correspond to Sandler's delineation of the necessary background for survival and continued growth.

Kohut described the vicissitudes of idealization in some individuals who embark on a lifelong search for an ideal other, a person who can and will fill in for the now-missing parental ideal. Those individuals who suffer are those for whom there has been a too-soon break with and loss of this supporting connection. Kohut delineated a series of psychological catastrophes that would follow from this particular form of trauma. He preferred to speak of drive regulation and channeling, of superego formation, of internal values and goals, and somewhere the idea of safety got lost. It was transferred to a personal feeling of strength and confidence, but one suspects that it lies more in Sandler's notion of a background that should be present in us all. The failure of this background may result in the cynic who has little trust or confidence in the world, or in the anxious person who lives in a fearful world.

Sandler (1960) also suggested how disavowal came to play a role in our need to feel safe. He writes that "the modification of perception . . . [is a] deliberate and purposive behavioral manipulation of the external world [in order to] subject the sense organs to altered and different stimulants" (p. 354). These modifications are used to have one's external reality changed so as to reduce anxiety. I have elsewhere suggested that the necessary role of the idealized selfobject vis-à-vis the environment and the traumas visited on the child becomes based on certain crucial qualities invested in the parents (Goldberg, 1988). These qualities are those of predictability, dependability, and reliability.

> The child must be able to anticipate the parent and so develop a feeling of a predictable world. The child must feel that the parent can be counted on and so is dependable. And the parent must evidence the posture of stability and so insure reliability. No doubt these words are easily interchangeable, but the kind of linkage that guards against disappointment is one of such predictability and reliability [p. 69].

I would now add that the connection that guards against anxiety is perhaps more closely linked to dependability. In the detailed examination of the idealized selfobject and its inevitable failures, we see what the parent was really like, and we can thus determine what was offered to the child and what denied. This background of safety, which may be a synonym for a secure and stable self, derives from the predictable, reliable, and dependable adult.

The patient Fritz did not have this or, perhaps better said, he did not have it for long enough. Thus his world became unpredictable no matter how hard he tried to control it; it was unreliable because he felt that he could not count on his parents; and, sadly, the entire network of his relationships was not dependable. Interestingly, Fritz also had an overwhelming fear of flying, simply because he could not allow himself to feel safe in the hands of another. He knew for a fact that people were quite unable to live up to their promises, and he himself lived this out in his treatment. His transference dictated and so realized a therapist who would never acknowledge his own deficiencies, but who could not really help, either. It would be foolhardy for Fritz fully to trust someone else, because he and he alone was able to care for himself. He was cynical. He was hyperalert to others' deficiencies, and he was ultimately anxious. Once again we may compare Fritz to a patient with panic attacks, save for the fact that Fritz knew exactly what brought them about and how to end them.

Let us put the two parts of Fritz side by side as indeed they seem to exist in actuality. The one is competent, self-assured, and fairly content as long as his world is enclosed within an arena in which he feels that he can control and regulate. As long as he can operate within this world, he feels secure and free from anxiety. But let there be a breach in the wall that he has constructed, a beginning breakdown of the stability that he requires, and he must face the other world of uncertainty with its associated failures in predictability, reliability, and dependability. In a sense, this latter world has always been there, waiting in the wings, but Fritz has kept it at bay by disavowing it. As Sandler said, he has had a deliberate and purposeful modification of his perception, which may be no more than saying that he is able to be temporarily blind to certain events of his life. These conditions were the substance of his childhood as he, along with his father and mother, lived in both worlds and tried to keep his anxiety at bay with this act of blindness. But, this act of blindness could not work forever, and so he became the anxious and untrusting child and adult. This mental state never completely took over his life for long but rather managed to express and spend itself and then, by way of an act of disavowal, be put aside for a time.

The question arises as to whether this condition of disavowal, with its shelving of a certain set of feelings, is peculiar to a certain group of persons such as Fritz, or whether it has a more general and perhaps even universal appeal. If it is the former, then perhaps we can better delineate the special circumstances that occasion its development. If it is the latter, do we not run the risk of making it so common as to trivialize it by simply noting that it is some variant of the ordinary ambivalence that was noted at the beginning of the inquiry? The addition of another facet of parental participation may allow for a better answer to that question.

The example of our patient Fritz centered around his vision of his parents and the way these two chose or felt forced to perceive and live in the world. Some psychoanalysts would consider this to be an example of the boy's identification with the attitudes of his father and mother and thus of his adoption of their viewpoint as well as their values and goals (i.e., he was a miniaturized and dually shaped version of the parents' psyches). Fritz sees them, and so he becomes them by way of internalization and a setting up of their representatives within him. This identification results, however, in a torn or severed psyche, inasmuch as these parents are themselves so separated. The identification is a nonintegrated parental model, because the parents themselves disavow reality. But now let us consider adding another perspective that involves how these parents perceived their son to determine if that suggests a further dimension to the development of his disavowal. Not only does this boy identify with his parents, but he also becomes affirmed by them through certain attributes or parts of him being mirrored or approved while other aspects are squelched or condemned. Fritz's development is a product of what the parents are, along with what they hope Fritz will become. Sometimes, in some persons, these viewpoints coalesce nicely, and sometimes they do not. The anxious parent cannot hope for a calm child merely by wishing a calmness for the child, because the identification with the parent's own anxiety may not be easily erasable. The disparities between what I am and what I wish for you become another breeding ground for the implicit messages heard and seen by the developing child. These disparities have to do with what is expected of the child versus what he or she is capable of fulfilling. There is a powerful feedback mechanism at work with this dual task of constructing one's self as an amalgam of parental wishes and personal capacities.

A case example follows that presents another form of a disavowed or dissociated aspect of a person. The illustration demonstrates that the set of psychological feelings that are displaced and shelved may take a different form than that seen in Fritz.

Larry was the only child of a family that, according to him, worried about money persistently all through his life. His mother hardly ever left the house, but she did spend lots of time arranging jobs for her son to earn some extra money that was to be turned over to her. Father worked on commission as a salesman, and so his income was erratic. Added to the uncertainty of Father's earnings was the uncertainty of Father's veracity, because a haggling between Mother and Father over his income and its resultant availability for the family was a constant din. This lack of forthrightness of the father was reinforced by the fact that he was a gambler. Larry often went along with his dad to the racetrack or to the site of an occasional loan procurement or debt payment by the father. Larry clearly saw both of his parents as needy and demanding people who made their way in the world by deceit and chicanery. Larry was a vital player in their lives, and he recalled in great detail their fights as well as his place in a space between Mother and Father. Although Father was quite a pal to Larry, Mother seemed clearly to run the family and to have great plans for her son. There was little doubt in Larry's mind that his parents were never together, never able to see things in a unified way.

Larry was a promising child. He was bright and did well in school. He was attractive and even charming to people. He had developed a manner of being available and helpful and these attributes, along with an implicit stance of being a rather undemanding child, managed to endear him to many people, especially his teachers and others in positions of authority.

Larry recalls being singled out in school for certain special assignments that characterized him as being a bit more competent and trustworthy than his fellow pupils. Duties such as eraser cleaning or positions such as class monitor were Larry's without his asking and, as he now insists, without his wanting them. In fact, Larry describes himself as being caught, or, perhaps better, trapped in positions of responsibility for which he felt not only unwilling but overwhelmingly incapable. He routinely felt frightened by finding himself asked and expected to do things that he felt were beyond him both in school and at home. He complied but with little self-confidence. He cannot recall any of these tasks or assignments as pleasurable or comfortable; they were only to be finished and put behind him.

Coupled with this school feeling of being pushed beyond his wishes and capabilities was a much more painful and pernicious practice of his mother. Although one or two of these events stand out in Larry's mind as representative of what Mother did, Larry insists that they were commonplace. One example oft repeated by Larry involved an expected (and avoided) collector of debt appearing at the door to demand payment. Little Larry, at a very early age, would be sent out with an excuse, usually a lie, to wheedle his way out of paying. Larry remembers doing this when he was around six or seven years old, and especially of having to tell a newspaper boy who was around Larry's age that money would be there next week, or some such story. There can be little doubt that the feelings reported by Larry as an adult were the dominant ones he experienced as a child: profound humiliation accompanied by the conviction that he was confronted with tasks clearly beyond his age and abilities. He felt forced to be what he was not.

Larry managed to be admitted to and graduated eventually from a prestigious college and a professional school on the basis of his intelligence and his inviting personality. This was accomplished with little help from his family. His later marriage to a woman who very quickly fit into the role of someone who saw him as not providing enough money for her and their sons was a perpetual puzzle to Larry. He tried very hard. He took on extra jobs, but his spouse complained bitterly that he had not lived up to a promise that she had heard, but that he had never recalled having made. Larry admitted to an ever-present burden of responsibility both to his wife and to others, as he valiantly tried to satisfy all the demands made on him. He regularly and inexplicably found himself, however, in situations wherein he became quite angry, an unusual aspect of his ever-pleasing personality, and, in his own words, sounded very "whining and complaining." He did his best to keep these episodes of rage short-lived, but not until he went into psychotherapy did he do anything more than hope that they would pass away over time.

One example of such an occurrence was a simple order by phone for some underwear that came with a very slight error in the delivered product: a mere matter of not including a button. And so Larry was enraged at the next clerk, who ultimately turned him over to the manager. Larry was tormented at having to call and complain, and felt overwhelmed with befuddlement when the clerk who initially responded to his complaint said they would correct (their) mistake at a half-price charge to him. Larry felt enormous distress over having to speak later to a manager who indeed realized that the error in question was entirely the fault and obligation of the manufacturer. The idea of having to ask for something that was rightfully due him was disabling, whereas finding himself in an unfair position of having to provide for others was familiar. In this matter, Larry recreated for himself the life of unfairness that had so characterized his life as a child. He had an unbelievable string of unfortunate encounters with people who, while ostensibly hired or acquired to provide a service, would end up getting more out of Larry than anything he had received from them. And periodically, the other angry and demanding Larry would emerge as if in hiding and waiting. He could not understand how in the world so much could be expected from him, when he himself felt so needy and unable to offer very much to others. Nor could he comprehend how he could possibly justify how much he wanted for himself. That last posture was one that Larry felt to be quite foreign to him, and he wanted nothing to do with it. He wanted to disown completely the person who angrily insisted that he was abused and deserving. But that presence regularly reappeared and seemingly took over the "other" Larry, the neglected and overwhelmed child. In his treatment, Larry had no trouble in acknowledging that he was familiar with this aspect of himself, which was always with him and was hardly to be considered as unconscious as much as it was to be dismissed. It would thereby seem to qualify as what we have termed a disavowal of a parallel and split-off sector of the self.

Let us now, with Larry as with Fritz, once again put the two sides next to each other to see the nature of the disavowal in different pleasure aims, goals, and values in an effort better to understand their origin in the particular parental environment in which he developed. On one hand, he sees both parents as chronically deficient both in money and in emotional support. He identifies with a needy and demanding mother and an equally needy father. On the other hand, Larry does not allow himself to emulate these overt characteristics of his parents, and it is clear to all that Larry must appear able and confident despite his internal feelings of fearfulness and inadequacy. He is to present a certain face to the world. These two aspects of Larry are by no means unconscious and repressed; both are available to his conscious awareness, although they are also quite incompatible with each another. One must be disavowed, or better, must be placed aside for an expectable return visit. This reappearance of the anxious and needy person is seen at moments in Larry's life when a certain quantitative factor in his own needs and other people's demands tips the balance to allow his anger and demandingness to seize the moment. The emerging sector is seen negatively by the otherwise caring-for-others part and so is felt as alien and unwanted. That was the case in Larry's childhood, when he was forced to squelch his expectable and rightful needs in favor of those of his mother. No doubt there was a good deal of compensatory gratification of his grandiosity, as he played the role of the little man. This may well be the solidifying factor for the relative dominance of this sector of the self. It seems eminently clear, however, that Larry was not able to feel the safety and security of dependable parents. This failure to have a sustaining, supportive ideal with which to connect forced Larry to fall back on his own resources. With this move to the grandiose self of accomplishments, Larry must strive to become much more than he is in fact, and so his stance of competence is fragile and vulnerable. Larry can be seen as straddling two worlds: one of a frightened boy who feels unsafe and unsure with parents who offer him little strength or support, and the other of a competent and assured little man who feels fake and vulnerable as he is forced to care for others.

These two cases represent a modified version of a split different from that of the personality disorders and behavior disorders. One striking difference is that the appearance of the dissociated material is routinely felt as dysphoric and alien. The behavior disorders sometimes feel the split-off area as equally alien but usually the behavior is a pleasant and effective solution that only becomes condemned in retrospect. This is also true of the personality disorders, which may feel some degree of shame around, say, their blatant grandiosity, but it is equally compelling and effective. As the focus is directed more carefully on the origins of these difficulties a better perspective on their differences may be gained.

As with Fritz, there can be no argument about the developing child having an identification with both parents along with a reaction by the parents to the resulting identification. If the child can happily become like her parents with some degree of integration of both mother and father, *and* also have this resultant image be met with approval by the same, then we should see a union. This may result in a sense of solidity and accomplishment. If, however, there is a disparity between the parental positions about what they themselves are, along with a clear message of what the son and daughter should become, then the child is forced somehow to manage this clash. But one must now add one crucial element to this mix, and that is the overtones of the parents' communications to the child. Lying parents who demand truthfulness from children are paradigms of this quandary. Both Fritz and Larry had parents who could not reveal themselves to their children save by messages and signals that needed to remain hidden, unspoken, or openly denied. They were not parents who gave opposing but clear messages to the child any more than they gave hidden but similar ones. Rather, they gave both conflicting and subtle or hidden communications. This variant of the double bind (Bateson, 1972) is seen in all forms of pathology but now takes on a certain clarity and focus in these forms of splits.

If identification is defined as all the mental processes by which one individual becomes like another (Moore and Fine, 1990), then it surely needs an added component to explain how one further molds and shapes oneself to become the person that is expected to emerge as that individual. Not all children are welcomed as "chips off the old block." Add to this the fact that certain attributes (such as the femininity of some boys) are openly discouraged or condemned. It is no surprise and is not at all unusual that one must struggle with one or another sector of the self. It may not always be felicitous to say that one self is true and one is false (Winnicott, 1960) or to say that one self is in touch with reality and the other is not (Freud, 1927); rather, it should be noted that they exist in different worlds at different times and for different purposes. And so it might be prudent to launch an inquiry into the split according to these dimensions of reality, time, and purpose. One should be able to study populations through the particular moment that the disparate self emerges, the purpose or function—pleasurable or otherwise—that it serves, and the particular world configuration or social situation in which it thrives. Indeed, the entire consideration of the vertical split and disavowal as pathological or otherwise must be considered along multiple dimensions, lest one begin to say that such and such behavior is fine as long as it does not bother anyone or that some inexplicable endogenous factor brings about a periodic depression. The complexity of the components of any one person's self-organization does not regularly lend itself to a clear, integrated unity that can be studied and analyzed along the dimensions of the conflicts and motivations of that unity. For many, self-integration is illusory and for some of these persons its absence is the sine qua non of psychopathology.

The issue that has been focused on here is that of parental communication, which is subtle and covert but nevertheless telling. In the complex interplay between parent and child during the latter's development, the balance between the motivations or drives of the child and the responses of the parents through gratification and regulation must be understood. Sometimes the child feels fulfilled and connected, and at other times frustrated and abandoned. The need to have the one or the other often necessitates abandoning one, such as when the need to stay connected overrides certain forms of behavior, or when the desire for gratification forces one to disregard the role of the other. Psychoanalysis has traditionally concerned itself with the fate of the drives and traditionally reckons environmental factors to be secondary. Freud (1905) spoke of the complemental series in his own explanation, and observed that in this interplay of constitutional and environmental or accidental factors it is not easy to estimate the relative efficacy (p. 239). He went on to say that "definitive" effects result from traumatic experiences in childhood (p. 240). He continually emphasized that our limited knowledge of biological processes made it difficult adequately to understand normal and pathological conditions. In this way, he opened the question as to why any one person develops one condition rather than another, why one form of perverse or aberrant behavior is chosen over another, and why one form of handling psychic trauma such as disavowal is chosen over another such as repression. Constitution, trauma from the environment, and happenstance all seem to come together in ways that remain mysterious. Perhaps the mystery can be cleared up if we are able to clarify the degree and nature of the contribution of the parents in what they communicate, how the messages are transmitted, and especially how capable the child is of assimilating this information. The cases presented earlier were chosen as illustrative of the parental contributions and not as examples of the more severe pathological pictures which will be focused upon later. One needs to consider both the degree of parental contribution and the capacity of a vulnerable child to manage the journey to adulthood without a significant and possibly pathological split. By turning to a detailed examination of the development of these conditions, the inquiry can be pursued in greater detail.

Chapter 5

PSYCHOANALYTIC DEVELOPMENTAL CONSIDERATIONS

The previous discussion of some of the phenomena of the vertical split as it develops in childhood in an atmosphere that seems to initiate and condone it will now be filled out with psychoanalytic ideas pertinent to this development. These ideas begin with an overview that will illustrate some of the considerations relevant to the question of how any child manages to find his or her way in the world and develop concepts of right and wrong along with values of personal significance and importance. There is no good consensus among investigators of child development as to the processes that direct and guide this journey to adulthood, but some psychoanalytic concepts may allow us to see what might result in the aberrant development that is seen in the vertical split. Two significant issues to be reckoned with are those devoted to the child's growing concept of reality and those centered on the child's sense of values and their attainment.

Reality

A child's conception of and relation to reality is explained differently, or perhaps better said, has a different emphasis according to different disciplines. These range from an "innate structure-program complex" said by Chomsky (in Piatelli-Palmarini, 1980) to consist of those rules or principles that determine what we are able to learn, on to a constructive view of mental development championed by Piaget (1954). The latter says that the child proceeds through a series of stages of cognitive development through which he or she assimilates new content and new meaning as he or she is successfully engaged in this process. Thus, in this perspective, the child is said to know the world both by physical interactions and by his or her presence in a social milieu. On one hand, Trevarthen (1982) argues that the human being possesses inborn systems that integrate interpersonal and practical areas together from the very first months after birth. Vygotsky (1986), on the other hand, emphasizes the necessary presence of another as a mediator of reality. It would be oversimplification to assert that these ideas are all of one piece, inasmuch as the guiding principles of one are at odds with those of another. Innateness is a perspective different from mutual construction. Inborn processes take center stage in the former perspective, whereas care givers do so in the latter.

Innateness insists that the human brain has deep inborn structures and is wired according to a given program that becomes activated by, and proceeds to interact with, an appropriate environment. The rules of language acquisition connect to the particular form and content of a given language so that the emerging capacity of the child to speak either Chinese or Portuguese is essentially constrained and thus formed by these deep inborn sets of directions or structures. The child is not capable of developing a language or speaking in a manner that defies these constraints. No matter how complex or simple the resulting language, there remains the rather strict and formal principles of the deep structure. Because our language enables us to connect with others, it would seem that our construction of our world follows from and on these deep, innate, and essentially unmodifiable structures. We follow a program with which we are born, and our differences may be less profound than we may think.

In contrast with innateness, the constructivist approach seems at first to even the playing field. The child, according to Piaget, does indeed have a series of inborn programs by which he or she discovers the world. The four main stages of cognitive development—sensorimotor, preoperational, concrete operational, and hypothetico-deductive or formal operational—lead to schemas capable of assimilating new content and meaning. Piaget adds the activity of reflecting to these operations, and this then allows for new operations. Despite the originality of the concept, there remains a tendency to allow all children to construct a common reality (Arbib and Hesse, 1986, p. 48) and therefore to arrive at a certain sameness.

The individuality of a child's construction and conceptualization of reality is perhaps better realized by those cognitive psychologists who emphasize interaction, and who thereby promote representations as the building blocks of the mind (Cummings, 1989). These representations are mental stand-ins for the composition of the world. Each child has a different set of experiences, and so he or she individually forms a personal and private world. Of course, this does not exclude the inherent constraints or programs that one is born with, but the emphasis shifts from a program that constrains and controls to one that is flexible enough to encompass a wide range of possibilities. The resulting construction of reality by the child is more variable, and thus every child has an individual version of the world. We move from innateness to flexibility, from sameness to individuality.

The introduction of nonlinear, dynamic systems into our thinking about development allows even more for the recognition of distinct individual differences. A nonlinear system is one that has significant responses to miniscule changes, demonstrates emergent properties from elements that do not themselves contain that property, and in which the size of the input does not determine the size of the output. Thus, in our examples of people who may manifest one or another kind of behavior, we must allow for the unpredictability of the phenomena. We thereby rely more on descriptive efforts than on linear causal explanations, because the cause-effect sequence might better fit linear systems. With nonlinear systems, one can never determine beforehand the fate of an individual based on the usual considerations of development but must rather allow for the person we see to be a product that can only be explained and understood in retrospect. Positing stages of development offers only a road map with no certain predictability.

The direction of today's thinking is clearly away from innate programs to highly individualized variability within a general framework of constraints or limitations. When we move on to a psychoanalytic frame of development, we may choose to follow the traditional analytic models that use ego and superego development to explain just how the child interacts with the world and learns how to cope with the world. Alternatively, we may employ the notion of self development, which places a different emphasis on development through the issue of narcissism, focusing on ambitions, goals, and their modification by way of parental interaction. I shall employ more of the latter with the full recognition that no single model captures the complexity of the subject. The goal will be to see how innate ideas of internal guiding programs become less significant as interactive models are invoked and dynamic systems seem to rule the day.

The Ideal

The mediator of reality, as first noted and emphasized by Vygotsky (1986), is considered by psychoanalysis in terms of the child's interaction with his or her parents. Whereas some cognitive psychologists merely note the impact of the social world, analysis has always focused primarily on the particulars of the parent-child relationship and has posited a number of mechanisms and procedures to explain just how and when a child captures the real world. Perhaps the first and foremost psychoanalyst to present his own sequence of the process was Sandor Ferenczi, who published his "Stages in the Development of the Sense of Reality" as his version of this problem (Ferenczi, 1913). Ferenczi, who coined the term "lines of development," focused on the change from a child's feeling of megalomania in reference to the recognition of natural forces (p. 218). The child feels in control of the world when megalomania dominates. The earliest feeling of total megalomania was called "the period of magical hallucinatory omnipotence" and was said to be seen in adults while dreaming and in pathology in the psychoses. This stage was followed by "the period of omnipotence by the help of magical gesture," a stage that has its adult counterpart in various magical rituals. The illusion of omnipotence begins to collapse as various failures are attendant on the child's disappointment in his or her magic. Ferenczi says this magical stage ends the child's primary narcissism and is followed by the assignment of omnipotence to parents who are thereby idealized. The period of magical gestures is followed by one of magical thoughts and words, and this is seen in adults suffering from obsessional neuroses. Only with the resolution of the Oedipus complex and the concomitant detachment from the parents is the reality principle said to dominate. The place of disavowal in this sequence is said to occur before the Oedipus complex is resolved, and it once again wards off traumatic external stimuli that threaten the child's pursuit of pleasure. It allows a perception of safety despite reality, which then gives way to a totally realistic worldview.

There are two main and quite significant steps that can be focused on in Ferenczi's line: the first is that of assigning power and reality to the parent(s) and so relinquishing its residence in oneself; the second is that of the deidealizing or debunking of the parent and a reassuming of one's self as the arbiter of reality, now with a more adaptive and realistic view of the world. Freud's presumption of a "purified pleasure ego" wherein everything pleasurable resides in the infant and all unpleasantness is attributed to the outside is, of course, a conjecture based on certain adult experiences. The projection of power to the parents is said to follow the recognized weaknesses of the child and, once again, is hypothesized by an adult experience of searching for godlike figures. There seems to be more empirical evidence to support the next point, that of the loss of the narcissistic overidealization of the parent occasioned by the recognition that the parent has failings, that the child can deceive the parent, and thus that the parent must no longer carry the message of reality (Kohut, 1971). Before relinquishing his belief in the omniscience and omnipotence of the parent, the child does everything to live up to the demands of the parent, to please the parent, to stay connected. This connection allows the imagined strength of the parent to be shared by the child.

A crucial dimension of the child's psychic growth is the next developmental step of the formation of psychic structures attributed to the reintrojection of the perfect parent (Kohut, 1971) in the form of an internal ego ideal. It is thus said that the ego ideal is a psychic structure that develops out of the original narcissism that was projected onto the parents and is then reintrojected in response to the parents' actual imperfections. An added contribution to this process is that of the narcissism's "passage through the parents" (p. 43). This latter is used to explain the modifications in the ego ideal, which varies from one person to the next because of both parental and cultural contributions. This ideal becomes the target for our lives and, along with the ego, serves as mediator of what we aim to become.

To recapitulate: The child's recognition of reality is brought about by a flexible-enough program activated by way of interaction with the objects of the world, along with relations with the parental figures of his or her life. Originally the child was satisfied and handled dissatisfaction by placing it outside of herself or himself. He or she also attributed powers to bring about satisfaction in her or his parents. The diminution in the belief in one's own abilities to achieve satisfaction coupled with the increasing awareness of the parents' limited power and wisdom leads to a more realistic vision of the world in which one lives. Of course, the retreats to wishful states of unreality are common and are said to allow us respites from a reality that may be harsh and difficult. For the most part, however, the gradual adaptation to reality allows us to see the world in what is often called objective rather than subjective terms. Reality, truth, and objectivity become hallmarks of adulthood.

Illustration

Some time ago I read of a foolish parent who reported on his following the rules of some religious sect which suggested that (for instance) a child not be warned of a potential burn from the eating of hot soup but rather should be allowed to try the soup and learn for himself that it was not to be eaten until cooler. I felt in my reading that the child's initial trust in the soup's being ready to eat was immediately and routinely transferred to the parent, who then became clearly untrustworthy for having failed to warn the child. The parent surely cannot avoid the assignment to be the mediator of reality to the child, and there is no clear and easy division between learning about the things of the world through interaction versus through parental instruction. The child who is burned by the soup does not limit his learning to facts about hot soup alone; he must join this bit of knowledge to a changed perception of his parents as well: perhaps one of betrayal, certainly one of unreliability. The parent certainly cannot take a leave of absence in allowing a child to confront his or her environment independently. Every bit of behavior becomes charged with a child's feeling of personal accomplishment along with parental recognition and appreciation.

As this child suffers the burn of his soup, he looks to the parent for some response for his suffering. Perhaps the parent feels both pleased that a lesson has been learned and sad that his child is hurt. The child's feeling of protection, the supposed passage of narcissism through the parent, seems to be offered at least two roads. The possibilities may be multiple but, at a minimum, the child feels divided into a part that says "he will look after me" and one that says "I must look after myself." "My father's pleasure at my burn indicates that he has some special knowledge, but his pained look indicates that he somehow let me down. If he were only one or the other I might know which way to go, but I seem now as one who is both disappointed and yet convinced of my father's power. Thus I become both partly realistic and partly committed to the fantasies. My split is born."

If the child has a parent who is not so divided, a different set of options occur. When the father is of one mind about the wisdom of his soup behavior and thus shows no remorse over his child's burned tongue, then the child may well be clear as to his disappointment in seeing his parent as a help, and then he may become totally self-reliant. This is both a traumatic deidealization of the parent and a concentration on one's own potential grandiosity. But no split may result. We may well be justified in attributing no such divide in the parent who may be foolish but yet may harbor no doubts about his position. Children seem capable of following the journey of their own feelings of rightful responses as the wishes for safety and security become less invested in the parent and more in oneself. But no child is free of his or her reading of the parent and the resulting reevaluation of parental protection and reliability.

The Superego

The changes in the narcissistic investment in the self as it traverses the attachment to and subsequent passage through the parent is said to end in one's personal goals and values as an endpoint of idealization. The corresponding endpoint for the narcissistic deployment of one's grandiosity is said to resolve in one's personal aims and a personal pride of accomplishment (Kohut, 1971). A certain group of patients is seen, however, that seem to carry a vertical split that goes beyond the mere existence of parallel sets of feelings in opposition. These are those individuals whose parallel personality goes on to *behave* in a manner in opposition to one's usual standards of correct behavior. They seem to be struggling with a total manifestation of the alien hand syndrome and so not only to be at odds with their own selves but to act in this manner as well. The acting-out of behavior ordinarily seen as unwanted or offensive originates from a sector of the personality not under the control of the usual prohibitions and restraints regularly and normally attributed to that person, that is, it is behavior that seems to have either escaped the scrutiny of one's superego or else is under the aegis of a markedly different superego. Thus the person pursues action that he or she would readily characterize as misbehavior or misconduct.

A rather common explanation of episodes of occasional misbehavior such as lying or stealing in an otherwise morally upright person has been to invoke superego lacunae or missing parts of one's superego (Johnson and Szurek, 1952). This explanation claims that there exist "holes" that allow for the passage of behavior that is not seen, noticed, or regulated by one's conscience. This is comparable to sociopaths, whose behavior is felt to proceed without benefit of conscience. But vertically split individuals do not regularly show attributes of sociopathy, a regular and routine expression of deviance that remains unified. Rather, the divided individual shows periodic and episodic displays of behavior that are felt to be obnoxious or offensive, and are certainly not integrated into the total personality. Once again, this behavior belongs to someone else. Indeed, for most misbehaving, vertically split individuals, the abhorrence of deviance is present, albeit in the parallel sector. Persons with superego lacunae or sociopaths have no such attitude toward their misbehavior. They evince degrees of misbehavior that are integrated within their personalities, and they do not themselves dislike these manifestations of misbehavior. Following are some examples of a split in the superego that is essentially a split in the self as well.

The Liar

Eric was in public relations and was quite proud of his ability to judge other people and to engage and influence them. This pride in his ease of relationships now and then suffered from his displays of somewhat randomly and unexpectedly lying to his employers and his friends. When Eric spoke to his therapist about his proclivity to lie, he initially defended and rationalized it and only some time later confessed that it was both shameful and essentially useless, because in retrospect he could see no earthly reason for his untruthfulness. It rarely seemed to change the course of events and usually seemed stupid and childish. But it came on him suddenly and frequently and for the moment seemed to make him feel good and even victorious.

Eric had no trouble connecting his propensity for telling lies to his father, whom he described as a braggart and blowhard. Eric remembered how, as a small boy, he would look up to and admire his father and especially the father's overt emphasis on a proper moral posture. Eric's dad laid claim to being honest and forthright, and also to demanding the same of his children, but this never held true. Eric readily learned that he himself could lie with impunity without anyone making very much of it. That is, no one made much of it save for Eric, who often agonized over these moral failures of his own. Father, on the other hand, seemed at ease with his own falsehoods, which left Eric puzzled and perturbed.

In his paper "Confusion of Tongues Between Adults and the Child" Ferenczi (1913) speaks of his patients' extensive sensitivity to his and other analysts' wishes, tendencies, whims, sympathies, and antipathies (p. 158), as he notes that patients see things that analysts cannot. They handle this discrepancy primarily by identifying with the analyst, and yet rarely make their observation conscious. This analytic situation is said by Ferenczi to be the same as that of the patient's childhood and leads one to see that the adult treats the child's play, for example, as if it were adult sexual passion. Ferenczi concentrated on the sexual and concluded that sexual behavior between an adult and a child forced the child to identify with the aggressor and so to be split—to be innocent and culpable at the same time (p. 162). In a more general sense Ferenczi spoke of the two parts of the personality: the alloplastic and the autoplastic, that is, the one that seems to react appropriately, and the one that mimics the adult. This broad generalization views the child as behaving much like the adult, in engaging in otherwise immoral behavior such as lying, while becoming an honest and moral person in tandem. This seemed to be the case with Eric, who resolved his puzzlement over the evident contradiction of his father by himself achieving a self of contradiction. Eric was not a carrier of lacunae in his superego, because he was a rather moral person for much of his life. The episodes of lying were manifestations of another Eric and could only be understood as his living out a very particular and special relationship to his father. Eric was certainly identified with his father, but he was also different in that he puzzled over that fatherlike part that arose in him without warning. The moments and specific initiators of such emerging selves are perhaps better seen in our next case.

The Bad Boy

Roger was an extremely successful salesman whose job demanded that he spend a good deal of time away from home. He regularly used the time away to get drunk and have sexual liaisons with call girls. This activity came to assume a greater and greater role in his life, until it was a rare weekend that did not occasion this sort of behavior. Roger was also regularly guilty over his weekend trysts, and he would experience severe remorse accompanied by a personal promise to forswear such aberrant conduct. He felt this remorse only in retrospect and not during his escapades. Not surprisingly, Roger's wife would find out about his misconduct periodically by searching through his credit card receipts. There then would follow scenes of blame and eventual forgiveness. He would insist that he would stop, or at least cut down on his drinking, and would most definitely never call for another prostitute. Roger would be fairly confident of managing to convince his wife of his newfound commitment to a virtuous life, but he also was himself confident of his ability to be well behaved, even if somewhat less convinced than his wife.

In Roger's treatment some interesting facts came out both about his involvement with call girls and about his drinking. The material came out over a lengthy period of time but will be condensed and reorganized in what follows. For a start, we learned that, initially, not every weekend demanded this behavior. Indeed, there were some weekends away with no such urge for a prostitute or a drink. Roger had originally insisted that only unsatisfactory sex with his wife forced him to seek out prostitutes, but a closer scrutiny of the events of the weekend and the particulars of the sexual activity seemed to show otherwise. In the very special relationship with the call girl, it was absolutely necessary that she applaud and appreciate Roger's sexual performance. It probably mattered little if she feigned such an acknowledgment of Roger's sexual success, but he would be devastated if the particular partner of the night failed to respond properly. He might then call for another prostitute, and soon the mystery of his efforts was erased, as his need for recognition and appreciation was seen as the motivator of his supposed desire. The sexual component was secondary to the pleasure of applause at his performance.

With this recognition of a need for applause, one could retrace the events that preceded his sexual activity to the contents of the day's work for Roger. And it became obvious that a truly successful day in his job would regularly eliminate any urge for an alcoholic evening with a call girl. The nature of the appreciation for his sales efforts was quite specific and over time intensified, but it could not be denied that there was a powerful correlation between job failure and sexual demands. This connection was not a simple one inasmuch as one crucial variable was the degree to which Roger anticipated success and the achievement of specific sales goals.

Roger's childhood allowed us an entry point for a more complete explanation of his sexual and alcoholic escapades, about which he afterward felt ashamed and overwhelmed with self-loathing. Once again, it is necessary to reduce the complexity of a life narrative to demonstrate a few points. Roger's need for response and mirroring were met in his early life in a very erratic way, because his father was himself both absent and alcoholic. Roger, however, was a good boy, responsible for looking after his two younger brothers along with performing a number of other household duties and chores. One thing that stands out about his childhood was the fact that he was often severely punished for misbehavior, while his brothers were never ever so treated. Roger insists that his parents were overzealous in their use of the strap, but he is totally bewildered as to why he was singled out as the sole recipient of this action. His separateness from his siblings was also his specialness in responsibility and suffering.

In expounding on his childhood punishments, Roger said that they were delivered by his father with the prompting and goading of his mother. She would insist that Roger be whipped and would stand behind his father as the whipping was administered. This clarity of the role and position of the mother stands somewhat alone in Roger's assessment of his mother, who is otherwise a vague person, regularly described as a preoccupied and distant figure with few maternal and caregiving features.

Although Roger was a brilliant student, he was sent to second-rate schools and colleges, and, as an adult, asked his father why he had not been allowed to attend a prestigious Ivy League school. The father said that they never thought of it. Roger continues to feel bewilderment at his parents' perception of him, inasmuch as he is clearly the outstanding member of the family, one who now spends rather lavishly on his parents and siblings, even though he persistently feels a void in his life from not being recognized and appreciated by them.

It was rather easy for Roger to transpose the events of his childhood into the scenario of his split-off life of the weekends away. He seemed to move to a scene of a proud and accomplished child fueled by feelings of significance and needing a properly mirroring and appreciative response. This was the Roger of propriety, dignity, and morality. Indeed, if he received the appropriate accolades, he was content and satisfied. This is the realistic sector. The need was intense and often unsatisfied, however, and so Roger moved into the sexual sphere where there ensued a sort of sexual pantomime of his psychological needs and state. He would perform, he would be vigorously responded to, he would feel relieved, and, later, he would be punished. In truth, his later punishment would and could reconnect him to his out-of-reach mother, who remained visibly in the background during his beatings. As an adult, Roger's wife appropriately served as a parental surrogate who vociferously lambasted him for his failings as a proper and reliable husband. In each sector of Roger we see a similar psychological dynamic focused on a wish for responsiveness to his grandiosity. In one sector it is grounded in reality; in the parallel sector, it is sexualized.

Roger acknowledged that what he did was wrong, but he rationalized it as resulting from an intense sexual need coupled with a rather asexual wife. The drinking allowed him to pursue his sexual urges, but soon that too became an area of guilt along with a struggle to abstain. Roger never drank while at work, and thus he maintained a clear separation between his weekday life in which he was a good worker, husband, and father, and his weekend escapades. In fact, Roger was one of those patients who felt that he was another person while indulging in his activities of shame.

One could easily evaluate Roger's superego as exemplary in his personal consideration of good conduct. Whereas in some individuals the agreement as to right and wrong seems mere lip service, Roger seemed genuinely sorry about his misdeeds, but again only in retrospect. He was also genuinely remorseful when he was discovered by his wife and subsequently verbally flogged. His heartfelt promise to reform and behave could hardly have been dismissed unless and until one had heard it said often enough previously. Only someone acquainted with both sides of Roger would conclude that he seemed to operate with two superegos, but all the while being able to maintain a clear knowledge of what he believed to be right and just. Indeed, Roger seemed, more often than not, to need to be a bad boy in his adulthood just as he had been as a child.

The Idealization of the Superego

For some time psychoanalysis, in its use of theoretical terms, aimed to separate the ego ideal from the superego or else to consider the ego ideal as a part or section of the superego. The latter contained the prohibitions and was derived from the parent's firmly frustrating the child's drives. It developed by a passage of the child's hostility or aggression through the parent, and afterward by its reintrojection into the child as a separate psychic structure. Whereas this superego contained the nos and the nots, the ego ideal was the site of standards and goals, that is, the shoulds and woulds. This neat division dominated analytic thinking for most of the period from Freud through Hartmann. There has always been a good deal of anthropomorphizing of the superego, which, as a homunculus, has been assigned qualities of harshness or benignness echoing its source in an identification with the parents. The advent of ego psychology led to many debates as to whether to assign one or another particular function such as self-reflection or self-control to the ego or superego. Sometimes these discussions sounded like real concerns over a proper assignment, and unfortunately they led some psychoanalysts further down the road to confusing concepts with material entities. It still seems reasonable, however, to wonder just how one's feelings of right and wrong become formed and subsequently fortified by feeling good and happy about doing what is felt to be right. When one adds a correct and accurate perception of the world, an ego function, to this mix then we join reality and correctness and so achieve something approaching a standard of behavior.

Vertically split individuals seem to carry different or disparate or contradictory standards of behavior. One part feels differently than the other about the world and how one fits into it. This in no way diminishes the significance of unconscious issues that many analysts feel compose much of the superego and its contents. Rather, it is meant to focus on the personal satisfaction or narcissistic qualities attendant on one's feelings and behavior. In the behavior disorders one plainly sees the disparity between the superego of each sector. In the personality disorders, this disparity is less apparent. Following is an example of the latter.

The Braggart

Howard was a middle-aged real estate investor who immediately let it be known to everyone who would listen that he was extremely rich and also intimate with a number of important people. He came for treatment on the insistence of his wife, who felt that his selfish behavior had driven her to the brink of divorce. She insisted that he give her more time and attention, because she had been enslaved to his demandingness for much of their marriage. He did not argue this point, nor did he feel it to be much of a problem.

Howard was loud and boisterous and took a while to settle down in psychotherapy. A single incident in his life will demonstrate some of the attributes of his narcissistic personality disorder. The incident occurred when Howard's cardiologist decided to have him undergo a 24-hour electrocardiogram by wearing a monitor to record his heart activity. Howard had a family history of heart trouble—his father had had a myocardial infarction in his 40s and died in his 50s—and himself had episodes of irregular heart rhythms. He needed to stop by the hospital to pick up the monitor for his heart examination, but on arriving he was asked to wait. He burst into a rage at the innocent and unsuspecting attendants and stormed out with a series of threats. When he reported this incident to his therapist, he felt what could be described as a slight twinge of shame along with a detailed rationalization that justified his outburst. This behavior of Howard's arose from the same dynamics of unbridled grandiosity as was characteristic of his regular personality but was a raw and unneutralized version that lived in a parallel sector. It was not associated with the dysphoria or segregation that we have described in those earlier-illustrated sporadic dissociated states, nor was it a split-off sector that would qualify as the misbehavior seen in addictions, delinquencies, and perversions. Rather, Howard suffered from a narcissistic personality disorder; his vertical split was a naked expression of fantasies attributed to narcissistic issues (i.e., megalomania and overidealization). Our earlier cases of misbehavior illustrated by Eric and Roger were behavior disorders. It is sometimes but not always true that patients with behavior disorders are guilty about their misdeeds, whereas patients with personality disorders are shameful about their displays.

Both Eric and Roger in our preceding examples seemed to behave in immoral ways: one in lying and the other in infidelity. These split-off sectors appeared to be characterized by an absence of a conscience or a set of rules of propriety, but they seemed to offer a heightened sense of self-importance or self-worth. That is to say, these individuals, in the misbehaving sector, cared not for doing the right thing. The parallel part of their personality or self, however, seemed to be able to behave properly, although in that sector they had no opportunity to feel pride or fulfillment by such proper conduct. That is to say, these sectors did not care very much for having done the right thing. To some extent, Eric and Roger seemed not to idealize their superegos. They knew what was right but could not always do it. Howard, on the other hand, had no problem with right and wrong; his problem was with other people.

No doubt there are many permutations and combinations to the admixture of ideals and prohibitions, of having personal satisfaction in living the life of correctness and properness. The usual psychoanalytic conceptualization of the superego as the arbiter of right and wrong with its concomitant affect of guilt (or shame) is insufficient in its explanation of proper behavior, inasmuch as people do things for reasons other than to avoid feeling bad. That avoidance of guilt must be joined with an enhanced feeling of personal satisfaction, or living up to one's goals and values. And the bearer of a vertical split is someone who often lives out a struggle over doing what is right and feeling right about what one does indeed do.

Two Forms of the Split

The preceding sketch of some of the origins and ways of visualizing the vertical split allow us to differentiate two distinct forms within this category—the personality disorders and the behavior disorders—and distinguish both of them from our earlier category of dissociation. Essentially the difference between the former two is the difference between fantasy and behavior. The split-off sector in personality disorders becomes overwhelmed with fantasies that fulfill its unacceptable needs, whereas that in behavior disorders proceeds to act out its needs in one form or another, disguised or obvious, immoral or otherwise. The person with a narcissistic personality disorder may manifest, for example, a shy manner, but periodically he or she becomes excited and has fantasies that play out in the form of a grandiose and dominant personality. This overtaking of the ordinarily shy individual is sporadic and periodic but represents, for the individual, someone and something out of the ordinary. He or she is restrained from much overt behavior, but at times the grandiosity is expressed in an excited and overbearing demeanor. This alteration in the personality is in a strict sense behavioral, but it does not qualify for the appellation of a behavior disorder, which manifests action that is seen by society as aberrant or delinquent and is more heartily condemned than a personality disorder. Both narcissistic personality disorders and narcissistic behavior disorders show a split of verticality, but one is controllable and a bit embarrassing; the other defies the superego and is more likely severely shameful. For the moment, we shall put to the side those individuals who suffer from dysphoric splits characterized by anxiety or other painful affect states, as discussed earlier.

The attitude or stance that an individual feels toward his or her other side can be a product of shame if one's grandiosity is overwhelming, or guilt if one has transgressed against a standard maintained by the more realistic side, or disappointment if one has failed to live up to one's personal values. Sometimes an excited and agitated reaction to a feeling of specialness and importance leads the person to feel embarrassed and even humiliated, if in retrospect and recall he can see himself as pompous and overbearing. In more overt disorders of behavior it is not uncommon to record descriptions of disgust and overt revulsion over some conduct that defies one's own moral code. And certainly a great deal of disappointment accompanies and follows a feeling of "selling out" and giving in to a lesser form of conduct, thus diminishing one's own personal idea of the proper way to live.

In each of these ways we see the split that is formed and maintained by conflicts in ambitions, values, and standards. And in each of these we also see the interplay of these elements as they combine to produce a particular constellation of either behavior or presentation of character. The next point to be considered has to do with the initiation or advent of the split-off part (i.e., just when it makes an appearance). Inasmuch as we feel it is always available, it may seem paradoxical that it does not always make its presence known. We need to delineate further just what factor or factors bring about the outbreak of misbehavior.

The Question of Defense, Opportunity, or Deficit

One disavows something in the world that is too painful to contemplate. In this manner, a person can maintain a state of mental and emotional equilibrium and thus can fend off the discomfort inherent in an acknowledgment of the unacceptable fact that one faces. Freud described the action of the fetishist in this way (Freud, 1927), and most of the elaborations of disavowal treat it as an instance of a defense against a vision of the intolerable, that is, the little boy's recognition of the possibility of castration. Better to remove that offending part of the world than to allow the possibility of a much more dreaded and dreadful bodily removal. Although a great deal of emphasis was placed by Freud on the perception or recognition of some external reality, disavowal has by no means been restricted to that particular action. It does more than merely obliterate parts of the real word. If one recalls the case of Carol, who suffered from an eating disorder, we can see how she defended against the feeling of depression by her rush to the refrigerator. Although she had one episode ushered in by the impending loss of a friend, it seems more reasonable to say that her overeating managed mainly to forestall and ultimately obliterate her impending sadness. This conception of a split-off sector serving to defend against something or other has been extended to include percepts, affects, drives, identifications, and more. Essentially, the emergence of the "other" self has been seen to substitute for just about everything, and clearly many of these explanations are unarguably overgeneral.

This overgeneralization of the reason(s) for the emergence of the personality or behavior of the split-off sector is regularly reduced to the occurrence of an opportunity. Thus, people are said to lie, steal, and overeat because they have the chance to do so. The man who cross-dressed when his wife went off to visit her relatives was merely taking advantage of her absence to indulge his impulses. It is not always easy to ascertain what else, if anything, the absent wife means to this transvestite, because the previously-noted defensive function of the cross-dressing as a device to ward off depression can also be evoked here as an explanation. The pleasure that may be experienced with this activity or any other sort of intense behavior is able to *both* erase any potential depression and become something sought after in its own right. It is usually true at the onset of personality and behavior disorders, however, that they do not have the appearance of "when the cat's away, the mice will play." Without in any way dismissing the importance of opportunity, it does tend to reduce the problem to a generalized weakness of the person who merely jumps at opportunities to indulge.

The idea of weakness is, unsurprisingly, not one to be dismissed out of hand. Many persons who behave in an obnoxious manner or misbehave in acting out and unacceptable forms of behavior will indeed attribute their problem to something akin to weakness or a giving in to urges. Carol, the overeater, will readily claim that the physical presence of her husband does indeed seem to lessen her urges, and certainly those who have been involved in various 12-step programs will insist that the availability of a sponsor or someone to talk to can help them to control themselves. The idea of someone else serving as a source of strength is readily transformed into their serving as psychic structure, and self psychology has elaborated this point in explicating the other as a selfobject that buttresses or heals a weak or defective self-structure. Therefore, the emergence of the split-off sector can also be seen as a reaction to disconnection from loss of a supporting selfobject. The absent wife of the cross-dresser breaks the structural relationship that temporarily disorganizes the self. The activity of cross-dressing obliterates any feeling of loss by the substitution of an excited sexual substitute. If any depression does begin to emerge, it can last only until the appearance of the otherwise quiescent but lying-in-waiting self-structure; from that point on the action dominates the scene, and the disconnection is diminished and soon replaced.

Thus we see that the elements of defense, opportunity, and deficit all participate in one form or another in the onset of the otherwise silent or absent sector. This parallel other does, however, wait patiently on the shelf to be available as it is needed. The need may be seen in these elements, if we consider the particular nature of the supporting connection that is felt to be an essential structural component, and the loss of which—the disconnection—initiates a downward spiral that calls for the restitutive or reparative appearance of the otherwise disowned behavior and action. The needed relationship is broken, a loss is experienced, depression is immanent, and the opportunity presents itself to fill in the deficit. And if one examines the particular role or function that the component or selfobject plays, a reasonable relationship may be posited on the basis of the developmental considerations spelled out earlier. One may thereupon ask if the selfobject or supporting other may be seen in one form or another, that is, as an ideal or a mirror or a constraint.

To revisit Carol and her relationship with her mother along with what was seen in her struggle over control, both with herself and with others, allows one perhaps to visualize what the loss of her friend may have meant to her. The selfobject is always someone under the control of the self and its loss is necessarily experienced as a failure of this control. The selfobject also serves a particular function that, for Carol, was regulatory and could be assigned to one or more particular psychic structures. The loss and subsequent failure of regulation ushers in an affective quality of displeasure and promotes corresponding psychic discomfort. As long as Carol was with her mother and reading in the next room, she was fairly content. Periodically the equilibrium was disrupted, and she and her mother engaged in spats and more severe disagreements. The connection was maintained but was unstable and threatened. Once broken, the relationship to the mother moves to the struggle over eating. The painful affect is obliterated as action dominates the scene. Arguing manages to undo any hint of depression. The grandiosity of the self is unrestrained. The constraints are lifted only to return later in the form of guilt over the ingestion of food, and the powerful feelings of shame and humiliation dominate the failure to live up to one's ideals and values. The reentry of the selfobject can magically restore all of these lost functions and once again restore Carol's psychic equilibrium as she returns to the peace of reading on the couch with the nearby presence of her mother.

Reprise

Although psychoanalysis was long content to posit the ego as executor or mediator among id, superego, and reality, the use of a more open and dynamic system allows us to see the person as part of a network of relationships that are in constant interaction with one another. The child grows in this network by way of interaction with the world but never without a parental contribution to this interaction. No one learns about the real world following an innate program in an individual way. Rather, we continually monitor our lives by way of our parents and their surrogates, and this monitoring never ceases. No act is free of our evaluations as to whether the act is directed to achieving our ambitions and living up to our goals and values as derived from our parental heirs. Thus when we learn about the world, it is inevitably a personal world, shared and inhabited by others, all of whom also have personal meanings, that is to say that we necessarily have a self-interest in all of our relationships.

It is difficult for the child to assimilate and integrate the myriad of self-interests into a stable and unified whole, especially in the case of parental dissonance, and one very prominent result of a failed integration is a vertical split. This allows for a coexistence of parallel but disparate renditions of the world and of personal relations. One can sometimes live with the unpredictable and contradictory lessons learned in childhood from parents who delivered messages at odds with one another. More often than not these contradictions give rise to psychological difficulties. It is to these difficulties that we turn next.

PART 2

TREATMENT AND THE VERTICAL SPLIT

Life must be gathered if it is to be placed within the intention of genuine life. If my life cannot be grasped as a single totality, I could never hope it to be successful, complete.

— *Paul Ricoeur*

Chapter 6

INTRODUCTION

Thus far we have seen that the presence of a vertical split suggests a set of developmental considerations and presents some particular phenomenological elements. Before an investigation of the pathological picture of the split, it may be necessary to caution against its overuse, perhaps first and foremost by clearly stating just what the vertical split is not. Inasmuch as it is not uncommon to hear persons say that they are indecisive or uncertain, just as it is a frequent plaint that one or more persons is "in denial," one should take care not to attribute a meaningful psychological division to the superficial descriptions of such a separation or negation of the facts of everyday life. The take on the vertical split demands a division in depth, and a perspective on its pathology requires a divided sector in opposition (i.e., there is a conflict) and sometimes in dislike (i.e., the conflict is an unhappy one). The "other you" has origins in the psychological depths of the unconscious along with a parallel life of potentially conscious distress. This distress will characterize those individuals who demonstrate pathology. Just as we began with a call to distinguish the various kinds of ambivalence from a vertical split, so we now insist that the pathological phenomena associated with this split lay a similar claim to the presence of a structurally significant separation. There must be a separation with a difference. There is no doubt that a host of phenomena may appear to illustrate some sort of split, and there is a real danger that a too ready embrace of the phrase will lead to overuse and to an ultimate reduction to the trivial. True splits are both meaningful and painful.

Another quite common form of possible uncertainty about the existence of the vertical split can be seen in cases termed to be primitive or borderline personalities. Often these individuals claim to feel that they are either inhabited by many persons or controlled by a wide variety of separate beings. Without now entering into a more detailed discussion of multiple personalities, it may be said that a mere naming of aspects of one's personality or character should not be equated with an in-depth delineation of such a personality. Often, borderline patients seem to gain a certain feeling of stability by viewing aspects of their behavior as a discrete entity or person and assigning it a name. As intriguing as this may be in a treatment, it is more often the case that the individual is poorly organized overall, and thus the activity of naming is used to gain strength and control. The patient who enjoys calling himself by one name while pursuing one activity or set of feelings and another name when off in another direction does not have a bona fide vertical split. This is not to be seen as different aspects of a person but as two well-organized but opposed psychic configurations.

The side-by-side existence of separated but linked psychological configurations shows a variety of evaluations or examinations of the one by the other. For example, patients, with a distinct and walled-off dissociated "other" that periodically makes itself known along with a dysphoric affect will tell you that they dread the appearance of the panic or rage that overtakes them. They try to manage their lives anticipating the circumstances that need to be avoided, that is, those that will bring about the emergence of the dysphoria. This is less of an issue in the personality disorders. In the behavior disorders one can see a spectrum of the one side considering the other. Some substance abusers hardly give lip service to a dislike of their misdeeds, and some acts of perversion are condemned and regularly sentenced to oblivion. The array of these evaluations are perhaps best seen in the eating disorders. Some patients will say that they can hardly wait to binge; others hate themselves for their overindulgence. If we consider the split as a coexistence of parallel personalities, then it may not seem unusual that sometimes they tolerate one another and sometimes they are totally at odds.

Everything from the occasional moment of feeling torn, to the omnipresent state of not knowing just how one feels, lends itself to the predicament of isolating the true existence of a vertical split. That is why one must, for the most part, suspend a clinical decision until the split is considered in, and as a part of, a treatment situation. Only here can one comfortably say, by way of the transference and with the corroboration of the developmental history, that there does exist a set of opposing but parallel psychic configurations or personalities. No doubt, familiarity with the presenting problems of such persons will, over time, allow for a shorthand assumption of the likelihood, but ideally the display of the split in the unfolding transference remains the only true test. Building on the material described earlier, one should be able to follow the progress of a treatment in the appearance and handling of the split, and one should be able to make sense of this sequence in the particular developmental issues that are felt to be crucial in its formation. Thus, at the risk of being overly strict in the membership of this category, we can start to make some general claims about treatment. For a start, there is a need to look at one of the most common and challenging forms of the vertical split and its pathology: the problem of commitment.

We begin with this issue as an orientation to the treatment process, which, because of the split, involves a dual focus of the therapist on the capacity of patients to participate in treatment without holding back a significant part of themselves. Because a similar problem occurs with the therapist, this examination needs to be extended to include the issue of boundaries as well. The orientation here is to considerations of treatability rather than to those problems of boundary violations that focus on issues of the proper and ethical behavior of therapists.

Chapter 7

COMMITMENT AND BOUNDARIES

Commitment Conflicts and Staying Outside Treatment

When I took my first class in analytic technique, I was a candidate at an analytic institute that made much of what was called "the commitment conflicts," which were said to be common if not universal in patients who were beginning psychoanalytic therapy. This conflict, which focused on allowing oneself to participate fully in the analytic process, involved the fear of regression and its concomitant ills. One would be exposed, would be subject to the control of another person, and would thereby soon have to relinquish the supposed gains that accrued from being sick and having symptoms—if and when a real commitment were to be made to the process. Not surprisingly, such a commitment turned out regularly to comprise an accommodation to the requirements or demands of the analyst. These requirements were the framework of treatment, and they involved the rules and regulations of an analysis, including fees, times, and a host of other issues that were enlisted as analytic lore. Any rebellion or resistance to a fairly rapid accommodation to the requirements of the analyst raised the question of a commitment conflict and the resultant corresponding assumption that this was the primary resistance to be reckoned with and interpreted. Ordinarily most of the conflicts seemed to vanish with time and regular analytic confrontation about resistance. In retrospect, one can never be sure if the resistance vanished with interpretation or crumbled with compliance. What will be considered here is whether the appearance of conformity with the requirement of analysis was genuine, involving a unified self, or whether it was essentially a half-hearted compliance.

Patients with the split have a very necessary and essential, albeit unconscious, plan to enlist in treatment while still retaining their disavowed other sector. They can accomplish this by allowing only the one part, the sector that appears to be more realistic and committed, to participate in the treatment. They do this by a variety of maneuvers, most of which have to do with issues of attendance and the schedule. Seen most often in behavior disorders, the irregularity and chaos attendant on regular meetings is prominent and often almost unmanageable. This need not necessarily take the form of missed meetings as much as sheer lack of regularity and predictability. These patients ask for unusual hours, telephone sessions, shortened or elongated hours, or weekly renegotiation of hours. They are not to be pinned down. To be sure, it may seem as if there is a willful plan to defeat the treatment, but one is really dealing with someone of two minds.

Of course, it is foolish to try to generalize too much about any group of patients, but the one generalization that may be allowed here is that the previously-noted lack of regularity is encountered more often than not. The patient struggles with the presence of an aspect of himself or herself that cannot be acknowledged or be allowed a place of recognition in the treatment. Sometimes the patient is totally unrevealing about the split-off segment. Sometimes the patient speaks about it in terms of control and suppression, which may also lead to the unlikely and surprising disappearance of the problem. But more often than not, the problem manages to be kept outside of the therapeutic relationship or, more to the point, maintains a silent presence in the treatment without being openly seen and addressed by the therapist. The nature of this unnoticed and hidden participant in the treatment is the most significant clue to the manner in which the vertical split is maintained.

The degree of participation exercised by the therapist in the maintenance of the split-off and unrecognized sector remains an open question. The parallel blindness of the therapist, at times more immediately and readily than can be fathomed, is enlisted in a sort of conspiracy. Therapists may find themselves seduced into ignoring issues that might otherwise be a focus of attention. Missed hours and unspoken comments make for an area of non-recognition that is essential to the maintenance of the split. This collusion of the therapist in what is essentially a repetition of a developmental state is not to be thought of as belonging only to the patient or brought about only by the patient; rather, it is an adaptation to the particular readiness, or perhaps I should say capacity, of a particular therapist to cooperate in the alliance of this form of pathology.

The therapist's personal alliance to a commitment conflict has its own set of therapist reactions, which range from subtle complicity to overt behavior. No matter the particular form of the cooperation, it mainly keeps an aspect of the patient's psyche away from therapeutic examination and analytic intervention. It becomes woven into the ongoing enactments between patient and therapist and is subject to elaborate rationalizations, or excuses, or simple silence. Perhaps the best example of this last, the conspiracy of silence, can be seen in the area of boundary violations, the majority of which become either ignored or caught up in the furor over ethical and moral issues, into debates of right versus wrong, rather than leading to scrutiny of what is allowed to be split off and disavowed. At the start, there is a need to clarify just how and when the violation of a boundary occurs, what it means, and how it can remain in an area outside of treatment. Just as commitment conflicts seem to allow aspects of the patient to remain outside of treatment, so boundary violations have the therapist join the patient in that spatial distinction.

Case Illustrations

Terry was a married man who had regular but unpredictable impulses to exhibit his genitals to young girls. He had only been apprehended by legal authorities on one previous occasion before he came for treatment in this, his second experience of being caught. Terry had only the most negative things to say about his exhibitionism, which he insisted he wanted to end completely. The beginning of his treatment was marked by interruptions, cancellations, and missed appointments along with this sincere desire to be helped. One can evaluate this behavior in many ways ranging from reality issues, to a wish to defeat the treatment, to the irregularity itself being some form of communication. It did seem necessary for his therapist to be extremely flexible with Terry in these early days, until it could be clear as to just what lay behind this seeming disorganization.

Another patient, Clark, went shopping for various therapists until he could find one who would agree to sign his insurance statement for a mental disability. The therapist who agreed to do so said that he was convinced that this was the only way to get Clark into treatment, and also claimed that if he did not sign the forms, someone else would. This initial corrupt compliance of the therapist was not understood for quite some time later. For Clark and for Terry, the therapist acted in a movement of accommodation that could be readily put to the side.

To be sure, some patients do seem to conspire to keep a part of themselves hidden whereas some others seem completely oblivious to any conspiratorial intent. Some therapists find themselves consciously going along with an extraordinary request; others are shocked and surprised to find themselves duped into an agreement that offends their moral standards. As treatment unfolds one sees that the moral issue is not always the crucial one.

Boundaries as Preconditions

As a start there is a need to look at the practical role of boundaries versus the ethical and moral dimensions of the issue. It is not always clear just how we distinguish between the moral and the ethical. If we borrow from Ricoeur (1992), we may highlight the difference as being between that of norms and that of aims. The moral is to be considered what is good and normal and so lays claim to a universal status. It typically leads to the positing of rules of correct behavior. The ethical has to do with the aim or goal being pursued and so directs us to the proper way to live. Ricoeur feels that ethics therefore encompasses morality. To transpose this distinction to psychological treatment we might say that we have a variety of moral standards or norms to observe in dealing with patients, all the while having a goal or aim in mind as to what we consider best for an individual patient. We start treatment with what we feel is an integrated self with a clear aim. We behave in a certain way that we consider moral, but beyond that, we impose other standards to promote our treatment goals. It may not be wrong in and of itself to tell our patients personal matters about ourselves or to have a cup of coffee with them, but it may not promote the treatment to do so. In this case, it is clear that ethics includes and determines morality. On the other hand, some may say that certain (for some) morally offensive or repugnant behavior is truly in the patient's best interests. These dimensions become arenas for argument and disagreement, as first occurred between Freud and Ferenczi.

Putting those possibilities momentarily to the side, it seems prudent to consider the concern with boundaries as more properly belonging to ethical behavior. As such, boundaries are the allowable constraints within which to pursue our goals. This view is familiar to some analysts who recognize that certain perfectly normal forms of behavior such as sharing a cup of coffee are considered as breaches of proper analytic technique. It is less familiar to some therapists who feel that sharing a cup of coffee is so natural as to make us seem foolish to decline. The difference is a product of a plan: a plan of doing good. Therefore it may be more profitable to see boundaries as the conditions that allow the plan to proceed, and therefore as preconditions of the plan. With this in mind, one can begin to examine and clarify just what preconditions are necessary for just what therapeutic actions. Thus, mistakes in the recognition of boundaries are not necessarily moral failings, although they well may be, but they are necessarily technical errors. A reconsideration of boundaries as the precondition of effective therapeutic action moves them from the area of morality to that of pursuing an optimal treatment process: an ethical aim. Thus the therapists of Terry and Clark could be both seen as ethically sound, but only one would be considered morally correct.

What may at first seem a fairly easy and simple delineation of boundaries, that is, the analytic claim of neutrality, has been subject to recent reexamination (Renik, 1996) and is held by some to be untenable and even unusable. It seems more to the point, however, to observe that supposed neutrality is for some but a synonym for the respect of boundaries. Little is gained by the substitution of phrases, until we spell out just what is ethically demanded of us.

The traditional image of neutrality or, what has been an acceptable substitute definition, that of staying equidistant from the id, the ego, and the superego, is an image of immobility: refraining so that the analyst per se does not make a difference. The usual image of boundaries involves an allowance of action or sometimes even encouraging action up to a point. Therapeutic action makes a difference. The difference between being neutral and operating within a boundary represents a shift in our thinking about the requisite action of analysts and therapists, that is, what should or needs to be done to accomplish one's goals. Therapeutic alliance, rapport, empathy, a host of recommended stances all speak to our doing or being something that is needed, rather than our being something that does not get in the way. It is the issue of doing too much or too little or doing something mistakenly that the issue of boundaries addresses. Perhaps one should therefore focus on the allowable and necessary actions of analysts and therapists rather than the usual concern with errors of commission. To return to ethics, we may say that we need to operate within an arena that allows us to accomplish our aims of treatment. This arena of operation assumes a recognition of norms and standards, but these norms do not determine the boundaries of the arena. Rather, it is bounded by what is needed to achieve the best interests of the patient. And often this requirement does not make itself known at the onset of treatment. This was the case in Terry's need to avoid regular appointments. Likewise, the "best interests" may not be discovered or determined until some time has passed in the treatment.

One needs more than a series of constraints to position oneself properly vis-à-vis a patient. What one *should* do is therefore more a matter of describing the conduct consistent with the identity of a caring and interested professional. All of the suggested guidelines seem to fail properly to define a boundary as a part of a treatment process rather than as a signpost of a moral failing. The effort herein is to consider the simple and perhaps obvious point of boundaries as preconditions.

What Is a Precondition?

A precondition is the sum of factors that allow one to effect a therapeutic intervention. It can be thought of as the stance or position of a therapist or analyst that should exist for him to proceed with whatever action is being considered. The ensuing action may then breach the boundary. There now begins the first hint of a potential split in the therapist. There is clearly no absolute point of effective intervention, and naturally the kind of intervention planned will determine the optimal sort of preconditions. There is surely an ideal precondition for certain forms of interpretation and for particular moments of optimal frustration or optimal gratification. One needs to study and define these ideal conditions to define better just what a boundary does and how it functions. Before one can possibly detail and describe boundary violations, it seems a wiser course to detail and describe the proper dimensions of a boundary, which seem to vary with the nature of the intervention that is being entertained. A therapist who, for example, believes in optimal gratification of a patient might well assume a different position than one who supports optimal frustration. A therapist who is planning to teach something to a patient will surely have a different set of preconditions than one who eschews a pedagogical role. Without in any way supporting or discouraging these particular stances, it is necessary to examine them more carefully before one can consider any particular action as a violation of a boundary. In this sense, one distinguishes between boundary crossings and boundary violations (Gabbard, 1995) in that one necessarily crosses boundaries in treatment but does not thereby commit a violation. The latter seems best to describe something injurious and in need of repair, and it insists on an ethical stance. It is not unusual, however, for us to cross a boundary unwittingly while rationalizing it as not being a violation, although it later turns out to be so.

Do Preconditions Differ?

A perhaps apocryphal story told about Freud describes his ending an analytic hour with Helene Deutsch and having her sit up. Freud is said to have explained to her then just what had transpired during the previous analytic hour. This rapid transition from analyst to teacher seemed to illustrate the altered conditions for his being the one rather than the other. His function as an analyst demanded of Freud a commitment to his own definition of neutrality (which may have been a liberal one), whereas his performance as an instructor may have been said to take advantage of a certain transference element that would lend strength to his educative efforts. Each of these positions implied a set of boundary conditions that, whatever the similarities, clearly differed from one another. As one considers the various actions attributed to analysts, it is difficult to insist on a single set of preconditions for what is now felt to be a range of activities that go beyond the single and most familiar one of interpretation. I call them preconditions because they are the necessary preexisting conditions that allow for the ensuing next move, one that may for some have interpretation as a final common pathway but for others entails a whole series of activities ranging from trial identification to instruction to more active involvement.

At the point of this "active involvement," one sees the step beyond the concept of a boundary as a precondition and enters the arena of actions that in themselves are held to be therapeutic. Often, boundary violations are rationalized as being in the patient's best interests, and so it may follow that a particular act can be seen as helpful to the patient. This rationalization then allows for the supposed violation to take its place as a part of the therapy. One does or does not do something to a patient for the patient's benefit. There is a host of such maneuvers that have been offered over time, from yelling at patients to hugging them, from scolding them to applauding them, from giving gifts to accepting them. All of these actions become anointed as part of the treatment rather than as violations of a boundary. And, as such, they are not seen as moral mistakes insofar as they are incorporated into one's ethical aim. Such actions lay claim to a status equal to that of analytic interpretation and so are defended as necessary. This rationalization is inevitably the major refuge for therapeutic misbehavior. It is therefore the crucial area for distinguishing the ethical from the moral viewpoint. It also becomes an illustrative dividing point for one to study the possibly divided or split therapist or analyst. This seems to be true for Clark's therapist, who began the treatment with a moral lapse.

For the most part, analysts take refuge in the principle of abstinence. Traditionally, this stemmed from the theoretical assumption that one must frustrate the instinctual drives to develop an interpretable transference. Brenner (1979), in espousing this principle, agrees that some gratification is inescapable, but he takes issue with the earlier claim of Stone that there are occasions when an analyst should give advice to a patient or offer condolences when a patient suffers a catastrophe. Brenner feels these actions are not in accord with good analytic practice. But surely, the failure to do so may be just as "gratifying of an unconscious infantile wish" as would be the offer. Neither position of an analyst is a guarantor of an ensuing successful interpretation. Brenner rightfully says, for example, that to express sympathy for a patient's loss of a loved one may make it more difficult for the patient to express pleasure over the loss. But to withhold sympathy seems equally to run a risk of a different sort. Indeed, there is no sure way of knowing what a specific action or inaction will lead to, especially because much of what is communicated remains unexpressed. Is it possible for one to feel sympathetic but withhold sympathy, and still remain within the bounds of effective interpretive work? Is it equally possible to feel unsympathetic yet offer sympathy, and then proceed to analyze the patient's reaction to the loss? It seems more likely that each position runs the risk of going outside the boundary required for effective interpretation.

Abstinence is no longer the insulated site for the conveying of insight, because the word seems to have lost its original meaning. Silence, all forms of withholding, all standards of anonymity, carry a powerful message that may convey more information than do talking, advising, and exposing. One must be very cautious in attributing a virtue to what is essentially a negative behavior. Not answering a question can create a condition that inhibits interpretation just as much as a prompt response. Abstinence as a form of the frustration of gratification can readily be seen, on occasion, as gratifying, just as action of many sorts is frustrating. Offering a tissue to a crying patient or refusing to do so speaks primarily to the therapist rather than to the theory of technique. There is no easy way to predict the effects of our involvement, and yet we are always involved. More often than we suspect, we allow ourselves to be split as to the nature of this involvement.

What seems to be true of most analysts and therapists is the construction of a particular individual boundary within which one lives and operates. This may be termed one's style, but here it refers to one's personal preconditions for therapeutic action. Given once again the usual moral norms, we all try to develop the optimal preconditions that allow us to be effective and efficient. Just as the taking of notes seems to work for some and to impede others, so too does an entire system develop that constitutes the most congenial setting within which a particular analyst-analysand pair can function. Indeed, the interesting work on matching of analyst and patient (Kantrowitz, 1996) seems to support the notion that a host of factors come together to allow for a workable dialogue. This notion leads naturally to the conclusion that not every patient will realize every transference possibility with every analyst or therapist. It also suggests that all sorts of behavior are allowable without any danger of indulging or conspiring with the patient or complying with the patient's distortions (Rangell, 1979, p. 93). But it seems to sketch out a picture of a therapist who must necessarily be split, if not with every patient then surely with some. The split of the therapist must somehow match or fit together with that of the patient, which proved to be the case with Clark and his therapist.

Noninterpretive Interventions

It is important at the outset to try to separate the usual and customary behavior of a therapist—what some would call his or her basic style—from those actions of the therapist felt to be responsive toward a particular patient. To be sure, some actions are felt necessarily to impinge on any patient, and so there remains a large fuzzy area that defies easy categorization. One would suppose that if one hugs every single patient, this behavior could become a matter of style just as much as never uttering a word could be seen as the same. But let us proceed to examine interventions that can be seen as moving out of the established set of conditions or boundaries to effect a change, just as an interpretation might optimally do.

Interventions felt to be therapeutic while not relying on insight usually fall under the broad category of the "relationship," or perhaps the "therapeutic relationship." That term is an umbrella for the variety of connections between persons. People connect or relate to one another according to different theoretical explanations. Object-relations theory may posit the relationship as gratifying a drive; other theories may see the relationship per se as providing a type of psychic structure. The benefits derived from these relationships encompass a range of psychological terms, from holding to nurturing to growth-enhancing. Most, if not all, of the benefits attributed to these relationships entail some scheme of development. Thus, a growth relationship may substitute for a failed development, enhance a defective development, or allow an arrested development to resume. Inasmuch as there exist variations in these concepts of development, there seems to be no agreed-upon set of explanations as to just why relationships are ameliorative. In the broadest sense, however, relationships are seen to function as supports or substitutes that are needed as a result of pathological development. A problem arises when one attempts to explain how a therapeutic relationship without the benefit of interpretive work can lead to a long-lasting improvement once the relationship has ended. That problem has bearing on the issue of boundaries as preconditions, because on one hand we assume that the relationship is some sort of vehicle for therapeutic change and so should be both clearly delineated and necessarily limited. Otherwise it runs the risk of being an unending relationship, a form of addiction. Or else it must have a mystical component that defies explanation. On the other hand, the disruption of the relationship accompanied by or followed by interpretive work is very much like the analytic situation of a bounded posture that allows for interpretation. As long as the relationship is able to be an object of study and examination it is able to be circumscribed and seen as if from the outside and so it is bounded. Unexamined or uninterpreted relationships seem boundless.

Relationships can be seen therefore as lying within extended boundaries. These boundaries can be effective over time yet capable of being terminated. The ending of these relationships can then be interpreted with hope for insight, or terminated in such a way that development proceeds, as is posited in the formation of psychic structure. The crucial variable would seem to be that the cessation of the relationship leads to a positive change. Something is felt to be offered by the relationship that leads to a long-lasting effect. With this in mind, one can reexamine the issue of boundaries as preconditions, that is, what sort of a relationship promotes a reasonable termination in which either insight or increased psychic structure results? This view distinguishes this category from transference cures and never-ending relationships. These last two, though not necessarily to be condemned, are variants of psychotherapy that call into question the very point of an ethical determination of what one considers best for a patient. The clearer category of a limited relationship, however, returns us to the notion of an individual boundary for an analyst or therapist from which one can operate *and* which one can terminate to the patient's benefit. Relationships therefore must be seen as temporary way stations, the very interruption of which can be used positively by the patient. Unless a therapeutic relationship can be dissipated by discussion, it tends to bind the patient to the therapist and the therapist to the patient. Therefore, for example, not offering condolences requires a discussion as to what fantasies this evoked in the patient, just as having a cup of coffee must also be seen as requiring a similar scrutiny. Nothing escapes the need for metacomments (i.e., for talking about what one just did). This scenario, which says that it matters not so much what you do but rather that it must then be examined, both redefines neutrality and gives us a powerful tool to delineate better our concept of boundaries. Without this delineation we are unable to see what needs to be studied, what needs to be noticed and attended to. Otherwise we run the risk of remaining split in cases where we choose to ignore certain considerations pertaining to the effectiveness of boundaries. But this decision to ignore is less the real culprit than our inability to see where we have colluded with a patient in a boundary crossing.

Transference and Boundaries

If boundaries are to be seen as the precondition for analysis or psychotherapy then the entrance into the area of therapeutic work, whether interpretive or noninterpretive, is an entrance into transference issues. Perhaps best emphasized by Gill (1979), the most reliable guide to the transference is what is actually going on in the analytic or therapeutic situation. Resolution of the transference can be seen as parallel to the resolution of the therapeutic relationship: the first by interpretation, the second by subjecting the relationship to the requirements of the therapist's own explanation of its value. Persistence of the transference, though recognized as ubiquitous by all analysts, is reluctantly accepted with a hoped-for ultimate diminution. Persistence of a therapeutic relationship falls under the category of a maneuver, such as encouraged by Basch (1995) in certain forms of psychotherapy, or else is to be otherwise explained. More often than not, this persistent relationship becomes the site of a host of boundary violations that are not in the best interests of the patient primarily because they reflect a wide variety of unacknowledged, unspoken, and unresolved transference issues. They become split off and put on the shelf or become permanent and rationalized enactments.

Once a commitment is made to examine all aspects of the analytic or therapeutic relationship, then no one part can be ignored. If a patient and therapist share a cup of coffee it must be made the center of inquiry. There may be little difference in an analyst asking a patient how she felt about his failure to offer condolences and a therapist asking what were the patient's fantasies during the coffee period. In each of these cases one attends to the actual reality of the analytic or therapeutic encounter and studies it for its transference implications. An inquiry, such as suggested by Brenner, to allow a patient to express his or her feelings about a recent loss essentially removes the analyst from the equation. The transference is therefore not the focus of this exchange, which amounts to an outside commentary about the patient. The same may occur with a variety of interactions in many therapeutic relations. A shared cup of coffee is not a moment outside of the treatment, and so it can be neither condemned nor promoted; rather, it must be made to participate in the treatment.

Unfortunately, many aspects of these relationships that are not interpreted or otherwise resolved fall into the category of being unresolvable or, better, are never discussed. Every such discussion of an event or encounter places a bracket around the event and so segregates it from the ongoing relationship. It says: "Let us step to the side to see just what transpired," and so, in its own way, it destroys the moment. It also recreates a boundary inquiry and investigation, and in this manner it alters the relationship. It thus seems obvious that *that* alteration is often the reason that these are undiscussed issues. Moments of physical contact, of self-revelation, of gift giving and gift receiving, of emotional outbursts, all tend to evolve into conspiracies of silence, of awkward efforts to erase or rationalize the possible misstep. Analysts who yell at their patients insist that this was for the patient's benefit. Therapists who accept gifts from their patients claim it to be a natural part of the relationship. In either case the event does not actively participate in the treatment either by understanding it or by supporting it by a reason outside of the therapist's own needs. Once again it must be noted that each of these supposed missteps has a right to be brought in as a natural part of an ongoing treatment as long as one can demonstrate that it is both necessary and temporary. And no one can easily distinguish between a defense of any such behavior presented as well planned or rationalized after the fact. The struggles of Ferenczi are an interesting study of that very uncertainty (Jones, 1957, p. 164). When Clark's therapist signed the insurance forms, that act should have become the center of the treatment.

The Problem of Relationships

A review of a provocative book entitled *When Boundaries Betray Us: Beyond Illusions of What Is Ethical in Therapy and Life*, written by Carter Heyward (1993), an Episcopal priest, is a fascinating entry into an examination of what seems to be a confusion about boundaries, morals, and ethics. In the book, Heyward tells her own story about her encounter with a female psychiatrist who, while agreeing to treat her, refused her request that they be friends. She goes on to say that this refusal was unethical and also a betrayal. The book reviewer disagrees and claims that the psychiatrist's error lay in not setting boundaries clearly and early. This reviewer, Marie Fortune, herself a minister and therapist, writes of the patient's mistaking a "healing" relationship for a peer relationship, and she assumes that the psychiatrist did not feel that a mutually intimate friendship was in Heyward's best interest (Fortune, 1994).

The published review article is followed by a response from Carter Heyward, who claims that she had indeed found just what she was looking for in her therapist who, at one point, agreed that only her professionalism was an obstacle to this mutually intimate relationship desired by the patient. Heyward goes on to say that this situation allows preset rules and codes to dictate what may not be in the best interests of these participants. Inasmuch as this particular psychiatrist said that she would have liked to have been her patient's friend, one may feel that the issue is clouded by countertransference, but in its own way, it is clarified by this frank admission of the therapist. Before discussing this issue, mention should be made of the reply by Marie Fortune to Carter Heyward. This last is a review of what is felt to be the respect of boundaries and a clear call to distinguish between professional relationships and intimate relationships. The plea is supported by an unarguable claim against exploitation of patients.

At first, one might quickly side with the reviewer who feels that this psychiatrist and her patient simply did not stick to the rules. An informed reader might well wonder, however, just why and how the need for this particular kind of relationship was understood and interpreted. As long as the wish to be a friend is taken as a potential violation rather than a symptom, it remains a part of the struggle between patient and therapist. And sadly, with no mention of the unconscious determinants of this particular wish, our reviewer seems to join in mistakenly considering this as a possible or potential boundary violation. One soon begins to side, however, with the forsaken patient who is never shown that relationships need not be either indulged or frustrated but rather must be understood. If the patient had had her wish fulfilled, she would have been just as violated as she was when it was frustrated.

The reason for the psychiatrist refusing the consideration to be Carter Heyward's future friend should *not* be seen as potential transgression; rather, it should be seen as an impediment to her understanding of what it means to the patient. The failure to explain adequately how one relationship differs from another (i.e., "healing" from "mutually intimate") stems from a barely concealed failure to understand what relationships are all about. This can only be solved by some sort of theoretical stance that squarely sees the relationship as a temporary place for a specific task. Regrettably, the word has itself gained a mystical aura that allows some therapists to impute an inherent "healing power" to relationships per se. With this claim, boundary problems seem inevitable, because some relationships seem morally correct whereas others are felt to be beyond moral norms. This misplaced judgment fails to say, however, if the relationship is a part of the treatment (i.e., is ethically correct). Being a friend is not immoral, but seeing it as a boundary violation blinds the reviewer and the psychiatrist from seeing it primarily as demanding an explanation rather than as a warning sign.

Therapist and patient placed to the side this knotty question of their respective assumptions about friendship. It never went away for either of them, but rather was split off from scrutiny. They joined in ignoring a segment of their respective psyches. This split then becomes the central issue that surrounds all of these unspoken and unresolved tacit agreements of conduct, whether they are seen as frustrations or indulgences. Not accepting a gift is really no different than accepting one. The unspoken always lives on in darkness.

Boundaries and Splits

Boundaries can be viewed either as practical roads to an end or as self-contained moral injunctions. There is a need to take a long-term view as to whether or not what is done will facilitate or impede the treatment, all the while accepting that some effects may not be capable of prediction.

Boundaries may be seen as launching pads for treatment. Their supposed violations are both inevitable and invaluable. When we step across a boundary, just as we move from one split-off segment to another, an enactment takes place, and we thereby change our relationship with our patient. If we extend the concept of enactment to include interpretation, then it may either lead to insight or else to a different position for both patient and therapist. We are unable to move from a neutral bounded place to interpret and then jump back to a safe neutrality, because the conditions have now been reset; sometimes a little and sometimes a lot. These new conditions become the boundary for the ensuing work. And just as every interpretation calls for rescrutiny of our position, so does every other sort of action or inaction. It is only the failure to recognize these resettings that allows for the prolonged realization of unresolved transference configurations and persistently untherapeutic relationships. Just as Sigmund Freud moved from analyst to teacher with Helene Deutsch, so too do we all inevitably modify our boundaries, and therefore we need to be aware of these ever-changing positions. Today, a supervisor might suggest to Freud that his mini-lecture to Deutsch be the focus of the next analytic hour. Nothing goes away, and everything counts. With this in mind we may see that the attention one must pay to boundaries is better seen as an ethical consideration (i.e., what is the best way to accomplish what this patient needs?) rather than a moral one (i.e., what have I done wrong?). All we have to rely on is our own nagging feeling of things that have been left unsaid. The best antidote to this ethical dilemma is our capacity to worry.

The monitoring of boundaries can be burdensome as well as painful. That would make clear, from an ethical point of view, why such things as physical contact, financial arrangements, and social interactions outside of treatment are often the ruination of analysis and therapy: they are much too complex for any one person to scrutinize and interpret. Only one's personal unresolved megalomania would allow one to have dinner with an analysand, owing not to the "moral" issue but rather to the general difficulty, indeed near impossibility, of so complicated a state of affairs being handled in a treatment. Certainly one cannot stay alert to all of the unconscious enactments (Hoffman, 1991) and shifting boundaries of an analysis or psychotherapy, but the clues to those relationships that remain unexamined and unexplained become available for study as one's own grandiosity is subjected to personal scrutiny and questioning. Therefore the effort to rationalize a boundary transgression is often designed to avoid the proper inquiry as to what it meant to the treatment process. It follows that we should limit our actions less on the basis of the violation of moral norms than on the very practical fact of our own limited capacity to understand all that goes on between ourselves and our patients, bearing in mind that "all that goes on" should mainly accrue to the benefit of the patient. Indeed, that is the best reason for regular hours with minimal changes: it allows us a better perception of what is aberrant, that is, not wrong but different.

The vertical split that is presented to us by some patients must, in some way, be joined by a similar split within the therapist. This union may be silent or open. We have seen that at times the split-off area remains totally outside of the treatment, which may be allowed or even encouraged by the therapist. In the case of commitment conflicts, the absent segment becomes a major concern of the treatment. In other cases, the split-off segment enters the treatment in the form of enactments that may violate certain moral principles. Here one notices the familiar boundary violations that are so prominent in discussions about ethical ways for therapists to behave (Gabbard, 1995). The split that is seen in the more overt boundary violations, however, gives us a viewpoint on a corresponding split in the analyst who struggles with finding a proper place to stand and a correct way to behave. Certainly not all of us have truly split psyches, but patients who have this divided structure seem covertly to demand a corresponding alteration in their therapists. Even more to the point, there *does* seem to be a split in those of us who, for want of a better term, seem to cross over, to claim that enactments are proper and healing. Is this a way that we integrate or heal ourselves, or is this an elaborate rationalization of aberrant behavior that triumphs over the split and claims correctness for the newly dominant self that silences the conflict? To answer this question properly, one must study how views of treatment have changed and how such change has been justified by some. We begin by examining a striking example of the split as seen in both patient and therapist.

Chapter 8

INFIDELITY: A PROTOTYPICAL VERTICAL SPLIT

Infidelity is a difficult concept to define as well as to isolate, inasmuch as it calls forth a host of moral and ethical reactions and entails a wide range of cultural considerations. Sitting as it does in a mixed field of evaluation, it once again becomes necessary to emphasize a psychoanalytic perspective and diagnosis. Although many students and scholars seem to guess at the incidence of extramarital affairs, which range from one-night stands to dual living arrangements, it may well be the case that no one really knows how common infidelity is, nor can we say that it has a unique and universal psychological meaning. There does, however, seem to be a special place for an understanding and investigation of the vertical split in this particular problem. Other psychoanalytic studies about infidelity concentrate on the fact that the person involved does indeed suffer from a psychological malady, and that the marital situation is a necessarily unhappy one (Strean, 1980). The sum and substance of these inquiries seems to be that such involved persons are immature or neurotic, and that psychological treatment is always indicated. The fact that certain cultures may allow or ignore sexual activity outside of marriage is not incorporated into a culture-bound concept of maturity, and thus all of those involved are ultimately considered as deviant.

The attempt here will be to isolate one particular psychological configuration seen in selected cases of infidelity. It may follow that all cases of infidelity in our culture bear a resemblance to these exemplars, or else further research might show that these few examples form a very narrow subtype. It is strikingly true, however, that the study of someone who cannot seem to maintain a loyal or monogamous relationship and who is regularly drawn to breaches of faithfulness is often pictured as a person divided. The division is one of a very precarious balance between two ways to behave and is then further characterized as the one being right and proper whereas the other comprises betrayal. The descriptions of infidelity often contain the words *victim* and *betrayer*, and so they regularly describe the condition as an act of disloyalty in which one has failed to maintain one's duty and obligation. Acts of infidelity nicely depict the vertical split as a division into right and wrong. It is well-nigh impossible to be "neutral" about infidelity, and as one enters into any particular story, one seems drawn into taking sides.

Once again, with no clear statistical evidence, it seems to be the case that infidelity becomes a focus of psychological inquiry when the offending person is exposed and discovered. We thereby see the betrayer as a patient, one who has misbehaved, and the victim as the wronged and usually enraged sufferer. The former is assigned the role of a patient along with that of guilty offender, and the latter becomes the recipient of sympathy and support. Most of the cases that come to our attention (and surely an enormous number do not) are those in which the unfaithful person has been discovered. We regularly learn about men who have been "found out" because of rather simple detective work involving mysterious credit card charges, unexplained telephone messages, and telltale signs of the presence of another woman. The simplicity of the investigative effort often makes one believe that a poorly camouflaged wish to be caught is at work. Only subsequent psychological study promises to reveal it to be because of guilt or a wish to relieve tension or both.

The corollary to the superficial efforts at disguise and concealment is the unwitting compliance of the supposed victim who often seems either terribly gullible and innocent, or, not surprisingly, a silent collaborator in the deceit. When and how the discovery of the infidelity is made could probably become a research project in its own right, because the anecdotal evidence is reported more as one or another crucial event—such as an inadvertent telephone message—rather than a long series of missed occasions of discovery. The wronged party is initially totally unable to see herself or himself as possibly contributing to the problem, and psychotherapeutic assistance to the aggrieved party is regularly limited to support and reassurance. The focus here will be on the treatment process that centers on the person seen as perpetrator, but this should not be taken to mean that the roles of betrayer and victim are necessarily fixed and thus associated with a parallel set of moral and ethical stances. Just as we know that every spouse of an alcoholic is somehow involved in that substance abuse, so too is every case of infidelity a network involving more than one individual. Just how a therapist fits into this network is often a complex issue that is not initially clear.

If we follow the path of one or more persons who enter treatment with the central issue of infidelity, we can begin to develop a picture of the vertical split as it is emerging and, if all goes well, engaged in a treatment. The following disguised cases demonstrate some of the possible outcomes in these therapeutic encounters.

Case Illustration 1

Dirk was a successful lawyer in his mid-30s who came hurriedly and somewhat frantically to see a psychoanalyst after being discovered by his wife in an ongoing affair with his secretary. The affair had been active for over a year, but had only been known to the wife when Dirk confessed it to her during an argument about the wife's sexual availability. An immediate visit to a marriage counselor was followed by a recommendation for individual treatment for both Dirk and his wife. This unhappy woman was so enraged at her husband that she threatened divorce and Dirk's permanent separation from the little daughter that he adored and could not bear to leave. As Dirk poured out his anguish and remorse to his newfound therapist, he confessed that such extramarital affairs were not uncommon in his life, nor was this the first time that he had seen a therapist. His last encounter with a psychiatrist had been very valuable to him, because he had been urged and had subsequently been able to resume his marriage both with a promise and a realization of fidelity for several years after several years' treatment. Indeed, he had phoned his previous therapist, now in another city, and had been told that he had merely "fallen off of his horse" and now had only to remount.

This latter suggestion was not quite what Dirk had in mind, because merely to return to his wife in monogamy seemed a dismal prospect. To leave her and his daughter, however, filled him with terror and despair. Of course, Dirk wanted both, but this ideal state of affairs was ended by his own action of confession. He had come to treatment to, in his words, solve once and for all his chronic state of unhappiness and associated infidelity. Or so he said. What he struggled with in his initial encounter with this analyst was a rapid alteration between a decision of leaving his wife for a fulfilling sexual relationship with his secretary, and an equally convincing declaration of committing himself to staying with his wife and daughter and "working on" his marriage to make it a happy one. Dirk was of two minds, but this was not a case of one hidden and one overt. Rather, they made alternating claims for control and dominance.

Dirk's analyst was convinced that a choice for Dirk of the secretary or the wife was presently untenable, and thus that an effort must be made to uncover his need for these parallel lives. In fact, the initial hours of interviews were characterized by each of these alternate postures of certainty and conviction. When Dirk would be confronted with the opposing lifestyle to whatever he had committed to for that day's conviction, he would readily dismiss that option as nothing he could want. His resolutions could vanish in a short time, however, and he would return to doubt and anxiety until the arrival of another moment of certainty. He could see no way to return to his wife, because she was seen only as a pleasant woman who had little interest in sex and who never initiated sexual activity. For a short time after this outbreak of mutual anxiety and distrust, she had become somewhat more passionate and physical, and this led to Dirk's decision to stay with her and his beloved daughter.

Inasmuch as Dirk was seen as someone who could not settle for an exclusive relationship with a woman, it was suggested that he enter analysis to understand better the origin and nature of his dilemma. He agreed but felt unable to commit himself to several years of treatment. In fact, he wondered if he could not reactivate the previous state of resolute decisiveness that followed his last course of treatment. He decided to call his previous therapist and return to the city that he had lived in during that course of treatment in order to undertake a brief period of therapy designed to return him to his state of marital fidelity. He thereupon dropped the idea of analysis and left for his renewed effort at suppressing his impulse to wander outside of his marriage.

Dirk is probably fated to repeat his infidelity when this latest effort at suppression has run its course. He had the unlucky draw of a psychiatrist who allied himself with a certain position of morality focused on monogamy. Dirk's infidelity was seen as a weakness and an indulgence, and the promise of a fulfilling marriage was able to be achieved primarily through an alteration in Dirk's psychology. Somehow Dirk was to view his perception of his wife as cold and nonphysical as an internal problem of his own, and thus one to be solved by a maturational process to be accomplished in treatment. This psychiatrist took sides, allied himself with a certain sense of propriety, and acted as if the other side of Dirk could be made to disappear.

The particular position and resulting behavior of this therapist allows one to consider the possible alternatives and their results. The basic point is that of the supposed neutrality or partiality of the psychiatrist. Either one believes that Dirk should stay with his wife or one believes that he should leave her, or else one believes that no decision is possible at this time. The first two are exactly what our patient struggles over, and the third is what he himself has been doing for quite some time. To adopt a neutral stance or to tell Dirk that one cannot possibly advise him as to a decision is probably the most painful thing that he can hear, because it throws him back to whatever forced him to confess to her in the first place. The advice from the original psychiatrist reflected that person's own judgment as to what was best for Dirk, based on what might have worked well for a while. We can thus imagine that the match between doctor and patient was a joint agreement to silence the wayward sector of Dirk's psyche—and, one would guess, a similar effort on the part of the doctor can be imagined.

Case Illustration 2

A quite different scenario unfolded for our next patient, whose own unfaithfulness was both longstanding and unrelieved. Fred had a lifelong history of multiple affairs and romances, most of which he had managed to continue without detection, although in a somewhat abbreviated fashion during his marital life. He had gone to see a psychiatrist because of a chronic dissatisfaction with his life, which he saw as one of endless effort and work with little joy and sense of fulfillment. This treatment seemed fairly satisfying to Fred until a crisis developed around his falling madly in love with one of his paramours. This was not the first time that this sort of head-over-heels passion had consumed Fred, but strangely enough it seemed to be more than his therapist felt that he could handle or understand. This psychiatrist, who had been helpful and available to him in psychotherapy, decided that now Fred must have a psychoanalysis and readily referred him to a colleague. The referral was made less with the aim of finally resolving this persistent need of his patient to see other women than with the intent of overcoming this present crisis of lovesickness and a possible divorce to which it might lead.

The transfer to the new therapist was accomplished with little difficulty, but the transition to an analysis did not proceed with similar ease. Most of that latter treatment became focused on the patient's erotomania, which dominated his life and the analytic hours (Goldberg, 1995, pp. 119–136). There seemed to be little accomplished as far as an analysis was concerned, but in time the acute agitation over his painful obsession with another woman seemed to subside. His marriage remained intact, and he insisted that his hours be reduced to conform with the schedule of his treatment with his previous therapist. Forces that were felt to be beyond the control of the analyst were dominating the treatment, and transference interpretations seemed to be futile. As the patient settled into a pattern that echoed his previous treatment, his own proclivity for regular extramarital affairs did become a topic of conversation. One day the patient reported that his previous therapist had been of a mind to tolerate such dalliances as long as he was careful and discrete. Now we had a quite different picture of a stance that allowed some recognition of the existence of a split-off sector by a therapist who had a different sense of neutrality. Fred said that his last therapist did not feel that these affairs were of much significance as long as they remained contained and controlled as to their impact on the rest of his life. The previous psychiatrist was seen as a man of tolerance and wisdom.

The further elaboration of this case can only be described as a stalemate with little evidence of a progressive deepening or much opportunity to deal with and interpret the transference. It is not necessary here to detail the manner in which some crucial information came to be known about Fred's previous treatment and his previous therapist's opinion about his occasional infidelity, but what did come to light, some time later, was the fact that this therapist was himself an unfaithful husband who had occasional extramarital affairs. He not only communicated his ideas about the acceptance of this sort of behavior, but also somehow kept this particular balance of the split both tolerable and alive. Now no one can possibly attribute Fred's original split to active encouragement by his therapist, but there does seem to be supporting evidence of a tacit system of communicating that was developed and maintained in that treatment. Perhaps one can begin to bring together the presence of a vertical split in a patient, a matching of this split in the therapist that corresponds to the previous collusion of the parents seen developmentally in this sort of phenomenon, and an implicit system of communication that is developed and understood by each of the participants.

What follows is conjecture, but it would seem that just as the parent requires a certain set of responses from the child, so, too, does the patient serve one or more needs of the therapist. Thus one can guess that the patient's regular but nondisruptive escapades with women outside of his marriage were a continuing comfort, reassurance, and encouragement to his therapist. Indeed, the therapist needed to have someone to help him maintain his own split at the same time as he rationalized it to himself. Matters unexpectedly got out of hand, however. The patient, for reasons that are beyond the scope of this particular presentation, became more than casually involved with one of his paramours, and his therapist became disconcerted as to the management of the treatment. He presumably referred the patient to regain his own emotional equilibrium. In retrospect, it was probably all for the best, but the particular sense of the "best" must elude us for now. Suffice it to say that the implicit recognition by both patient and therapist of their reciprocal psychological needs makes for a static state in some treatments. The disavowed material is acknowledged and quietly tolerated as a meeting of minds, albeit divided minds, is achieved.

These two cases are illustrative of the initiation of treatment in many cases of infidelity, and they demonstrate further our earlier comments on commitments and boundaries. Here one can see how patients allow themselves safe harbor by way of commitment to a treatment that will enable them to maintain their splits. It also needs to be noted how therapists betray their own psychological needs by an arrangement in which therapeutic boundaries are not established and maintained.

Caution must be exercised when we attribute conditions of moral laxness to therapists based on their patients' misbehavior. Imagine a continuum of therapists who range from the extremes of moral rectitude to those of moral laxness. Lining up our patients to meet their individual needs at some point along this continuum could surely be seen to make sense, because some patients might need some misbehavior to be tolerated and some to be condemned. So the patient would feel most understood by someone who could share their particular struggle. But it is not so easy. The therapist may feel that he has a clear position on some behavior such as infidelity, but he may himself have a disavowed sector about this issue as well. Some of our patients either evoke or help to suppress some of our own tendencies to misbehave. The therapist who is adamantly convinced about the correctness of any particular form of behavior is probably unable to help the split patient. The therapist who is equally convinced of a completely liberal position about the same form of behavior is equally of no use to the patient. Allowing *or* suppressing the behavior enlists the therapist in the same futile exercise of willpower versus freedom with which the patient is all too familiar. The proper position to understand the struggle is to know the struggle.

At the beginning of this book, I mentioned the case of the woman who stole from the supermarket. Her therapist told me that he had told her that he understood that she needed to do this, although he did not know why she did so. I asked him if he had himself ever wanted to steal food from a supermarket, and he laughed and said "certainly not." I admit that that answer surprised me a little because I myself have had that temptation fairly often. I had to tell him that I could not see how he could help that woman until he could get in touch with that wish in himself. He was dismayed.

It is not enough to condemn or condone a behavior, nor is it enough to comment on the behavior from afar. If the psychiatrist who told the patient to "get back on the horse" would say that he was able to contemplate infidelity and so to fight it, he would be of no help. One must somehow move to the middle, to know what it is and what it is like and yet not need to do it. I think that sums up my own supermarket morality.

We next turn to cases in which the analyst quickly recognized the patient's split along with the delicate balance that was required.

Each of the following cases demonstrates the absolute need of the patient for the disavowed material to be retained until a relationship becomes available which can, at least temporarily, absorb, connect to, or satisfy this separate sector. Sometimes this goal can be accomplished by a therapist in psychotherapy, or by the analyst in an analysis, or by happenstance. Such a connection often reveals the particular dynamic factors composing the split-off sector, and one may then routinely note the underlying distressing affect. It is essential for the split-off sector to become an active and recognized participant in the treatment process. Following is an example of such participations.

Case Illustration

Stan was a middle-aged car salesman whose frequenting of massage parlors, pornographic shops, and call girls was reported in a lengthy and somewhat colorful tale of life that he insisted was characterized by sexual addiction. He was used to all of the jargon and procedures connected to the ways of addiction, because some years earlier he had been involved both in psychotherapy and in a 12-step program for substance abuse, and he compared his present set of experiences to those that had earlier centered around alcohol and other pharmacological substances. He had recently attended a few group meetings devoted to handling these latter forms of sexual addiction, but he stumbled over the requirement that the members practice complete sexual abstinence save that of an intimate relationship with one's wife. Stan had convinced himself that his own personal sexual needs could not be accommodated in a strictly monogamous relationship, although he felt very strongly that he loved his wife and wanted to stay married. That seemed not always to be the case, however, because the idea of a divorce had occurred frequently to him. This last idea seemed to emerge in the context of an elaborate fantasy of a whole series of sexual activities involving multiple sexual partners. But no sooner would Stan talk about this imagined possibility than he would flip back to the very important place of his marriage in his life. Stan portrayed himself very clearly as someone who could perhaps control and contain his sexual indiscretions, but also as someone who was incapable of eliminating them from his life for anything more than a brief period.

Stan's back-and-forth position was dramatically brought to a head when he found himself deeply involved with a young woman who worked in a massage parlor that he frequented. They began seeing a good deal of each other outside of her work situation, which progressed to expressions of love and affection despite the fact that she was also married and a mother. As is so often the case in these matters, this woman inadvertently called him at a number to which his wife had access, and the whole affair became exposed. Stan came to yet another psychiatrist with an anxious worry of losing his marriage, and he coupled this new venture into treatment with both marital counseling and a reconnection to one or more groups devoted to problems of sexual addiction. It was an all-out press to push away an oncoming threat to the equilibrium that he had managed to achieve and maintain. He thereupon chose to enlist his present therapist in an effort to restore the balance of his life, but this was presented only as a wish to eradicate his current involvement with his newfound sexual partner. He made it clear in his beginning hours that he felt driven by his fantasies and behavior, and that he now wished to be free of them. He also could be heard to say, however, that he could not possibly allow that part of him to be permanently removed.

Stan's treatment had to recognize and appreciate the necessity of the split-off sector of his life. His own efforts at suppression could be seen as the swinging of a pendulum that could find no resting place. He would no sooner describe an intimate moment with his wife than he would follow it with a recounting of driving to the parking lot outside of the massage parlor to get a glimpse of his lost love. Initially it was the job of his treatment to point out how frightened he became following the intimacy with his wife, because it could signal total involvement with her and entrance into something that was both fearful and depriving; it could mean the end of a life of freedom. But the latter became just as foreboding and dangerous if it were allowed dominance. No matter how much one or the other sector could be seen as inviting and desirable, it could quickly provide the basis of a paralyzing and deprived existence. With this in mind, the therapist could aim to position himself in an equally divided fashion to appreciate the nature of Stan's dilemma and its concomitant suffering. Once this division was communicated to Stan, his anxiety markedly decreased and his puzzlement took center stage. He could not initially comprehend how he could be expected to maintain his balance of split sectors with the aim of ultimately dispensing with one or the other. This would require a critical appraisal and suppression of one of them. Each was a lifeline. He could not possibly extinguish either one.

When Stan's case was brought to supervision, it became clear to the therapist that he was both intrigued by the description of the sexual escapades and critical of Stan's wife, who was seen as harsh and critical. This stance of the therapist seemed to push Stan into a defiant and belligerent attitude toward his wife. With a reconsideration of this attitude toward Stan's wife, the therapist moved—albeit silently—to a closer alliance with the wife and a critical attitude toward Stan's "misconduct." This latter posture exposed, to a much greater depth than had been seen before, Stan's profound depression. This then became the fundamental issue to be resolved.

The parallel sectors of the unfaithful person can be said to be unfaithful to each other. The so-called rift in the ego, once thought to be separating a reality ego from a disowned and unacknowledged ego, can also be seen as a division into two realities. Each serves different ends, yet each has an importance, even an absolute necessity. One can only begin to understand the man or woman who must balance a disharmonious life if an effort is made to see what different purposes each reality serves. The balance that must be attained and maintained is that of sectors that have different aims and values yet share a common goal of maintaining psychic equilibrium. That equilibrium is best thought of as revolving around the regulation of self-esteem, and the switch from one sector to the other becomes much clearer and capable of explanation if we are able to follow a sequence involving self-vulnerability, self-imbalance, and self-restoration.

Seeing these splits as manifestations of disorders of narcissism begins to cast a ray of clarity. The next step in the therapy or analysis of the unfaithful patient is a delineation of the sequence involving a potential or real narcissistic injury, a turn to the disavowed sector for restorative action, a reconstitution of the fragile self, and the renewed disavowing of that sector until it is needed once again. Initially this is often accomplished in nontransference situations where one can observe oneself as if from the outside. The analyst is not to be taken as a proponent of one or another field of reality, but rather joins with the patient in following the series of situations that precede that action. It is usually following the explanation of this sequence that the vertical split as seen in infidelity begins to take up residence within the hour and in relation to the analyst. This sequence of extra-transferential to intratransferential should not be taken to mean that there is no initial transference at work. It is more a description of the direction that the treatment commonly takes. These treatments are initially consumed by tales of elaborate intrigues, but ultimately they do become centered entirely within the transference.

Cases of infidelity that seem to be resolved without an active participation of the split within the transference no doubt occur and may even be more prevalent than one can possibly know. The crucial point of such cases—at least those that are not simply efforts at control and suppression—is that they probably involve some real-life event that manages to satisfy one sector. The birth of a child may often be the singular happening that offers enough narcissistic balance to alleviate aberrant urges (or on the contrary can lead to an exacerbation of quiescent urges). A not uncommon phenomenon that is seen to follow in such spontaneously resolved lives of unfaithfulness is a chronic, low-level depression that seems to accompany the ex-betrayer. He or she "behaves" but is less active and often becomes morose. There is no doubt that one often sees hints of this depressive affect in many of these individuals, and the accompanying self-chastisement practiced after certain acts of extramarital self-indulgence can be seen as a self-punitive exercise aimed at relieving guilt. This self-loathing can also temporarily lessen the depression, and indeed some individuals become adept at a regular routine of personal name-calling. The use of pharmacological agents to relieve the depression is also a common treatment regimen that may precede or follow the successful effort to eliminate the infidelity. To properly understand the origin and maintenance of the split psyche that is so representative of patients with infidelity, however, it is necessary to study it as it unfolds in the transference situation in psychotherapy or psychoanalysis, because only then can one clarify the basic organization of the split. Although one can see the symptom of infidelity as representative of a split psyche, infidelity per se does not present an ideal example of effective dynamic treatment of the vertical split. For that we must turn to the numerous cases seen in practice and reported in the literature wherein the technical management of disavowal is discussed and the issues surrounding it are explained. As was seen previously in the illustrated cases, the entry into treatment is often signaled by a crisis and may not allow for an easy transition to psychoanalysis. Transitional modes of treatment may be employed, and each of them may make it difficult to get a clear picture of the vertical split and its transference configurations. Over time, however, there is often a settling down to a more stable therapeutic setting that allows for the crucial technical interventions.

Infidelity, with its characteristics of guilt and discovery, falls into the category of a behavior disorder, and the split here is apparent. It is less so in the personality disorders, and more subtle still in the painful dissociated states characterized by anxiety attacks. Not surprisingly, the treatment approaches call for different responses from the therapist, although they are similar in calling on the therapist to be attentive to the split. In the dysphoric states, therapists join with patients in looking negatively at the manifestations of painful states. The personality disorders run a range of responses, but as long as they remain in the arena of dreams and fantasies, they can be tolerated and interpreted with relative ease. But the behavior disorders stand out, because patients initially conceal them, and when they do participate in the transference, they tend to promote the blindness, often shared by patient and therapist, that accompanies the movement from ideation to action.

Chapter 9

SPECIFIC TREATMENT ISSUES
AND THE VERTICAL SPLIT

Our psychotherapeutic and psychoanalytic literature is filled with descriptions of patients whose major defensive mechanism is disavowal, those who present with a "rift in the ego" or a vertical split. Almost all of these case reports are presented with the picture of the therapist or analyst observing the patient from the outside and thereupon pointing out to the patient what is seen by the therapist as a break with reality, or a denial of a bit of reality, or perhaps a refusal to acknowledge some information conveyed to the patient by the analyst. More often than not, a certain recalcitrance on the part of the patient to agree with this appraisal leads to a frustrated and resentful therapist who seems called on to explain the unhappy state of affairs and may do so by an alteration of a theory of treatment.

In the earlier case of Fritz, his anxiety always occurred outside of treatment and was felt as totally foreign to him, as both he and the therapist saw it from outside. When and if the disavowed material does come into the treatment with this form of pathology, a set of thoughts and feelings eventually becomes directed toward the therapist; usually, however, the issue becomes problematic only if some unrecognized or mishandled countertransference becomes evident. It is the same with the treatment of the personality disorders, inasmuch as the integration of the disavowed material is still capable of being looked on (i.e., it is ideational and can be isolated and seen as a thing apart). It is different with the behavior disorders, because here the transference is often expressed in the form of behavior. That is to say, an enactment which is sometimes in the background comes to the fore. At times the therapist does act, and may even misbehave, hence the relevance of our earlier discussion on boundaries. At other times the therapist handles this wish to behave or "act in" by the construction of a new or altered theory that allows a certain kind of tolerable behavior for the therapist, which itself is often justified in this new theory construction or by way of rationalization. For example, one theory may recommend a particular emotion, such as optimism, be shown by the therapist, or else a particular maneuver such as sharing a cup of coffee is encouraged. It is unusual that this behavior of the therapist's is seen as the most important part of the treatment, save for those therapists who recommend providing a form of teaching or parenting as an essential part of treatment. For the most part, it is seen as trivial or as a part of acting naturally. Vertically split material tends to remain a thing apart. Although some enactment may be said to be going on, it is pushed to the side or ignored, and the therapist rarely focuses on it.

If a therapist cancels an appointment for a holiday or illness or some other unspoken reason, it is a commonplace for the therapist to wonder about what the patient may have thought about the missed hour. Some therapists wait to find out; others ask about it or even after a while are moved to ask just why no mention has been made of the absence. The therapeutic work is directed to an examination of the meaning to the patient of the missed appointment. If the patient denies the impact of the miss, then one infers the operation of denial or disavowal. Reality becomes the focus of the treatment. It is highly unusual for a therapist to recognize that his or her own feeling about the missed appointment is perhaps the most significant contribution to its full understanding. Therapists tend to concentrate on the patient's nonrecognition of the missed hour or its meaning, and so ignore the patient's possibly real recognition of a mutual enactment. The patient knows that the therapist has a reaction to the missed appointment but agrees at an unspoken level to leave it alone. This is not to say, however, that the sum and substance of the work is composed of this latter intersubjective mix. Neither is all open to discussion or all open to behavior. Some of the interaction is talked about and some is not.

The therapist who bemoans the fact that her interpretations come to naught as the transference is enacted or sexualized is unable to see that only half of the work is done. The patient has a reaction to the missed hour, and this is accompanied by some implicit knowledge on the patient's part that the therapist is reacting as well. The patient may talk about neither or one but rarely both, because therapists themselves prefer the one and sometimes the other but rarely both. Therapists usually focus on that sector of disavowed material that excludes their own participation; they may insist that the patient discuss what she and the therapist feel is central, which regularly excludes the activity of the therapist. Such cases are sometimes reported as representing patients filled with hostility or enacting a sadomasochistic relationship as the therapist persists and the patient resists. Theories are then spun about these patients' need to evoke hostility in the therapist. If the patient feels support and understanding, then the theory may become further employed or elaborated to avoid allowing the patient to attain a defensive illusion (Reed, 1997, p. 1176).

But the fact may be that the connection to a selfobject is the only way to heal the split, because interpretations to one or the other side usually manage to maintain the split. The patient who misses the hour needs to explore the fantasies about the miss along with the enactment of what might be a welcome return. The former may satisfy the reality sector, the latter the split-off action sector. The integration comes with a comment about both of them. If one discusses *only* the fantasies about the absence or the feelings about the enactment, then the other is effectively ignored and silenced. Every patient with a vertical split needs the recognition of each side. Unfortunately, therapists tend to pick one sector and therefore implicitly support the split.

None of this should be construed as making a claim for a new or revised approach to countertransference, which is surely the overarching concept for all of the therapeutic action that responds to the patient's transferences. Rather, we are aiming at a heightened awareness of the therapist's or analyst's splits that match those of the patient. The disavowed aspects of therapists usually have taken a subsidiary position to the feelings and actions that are ordinarily considered to be repressed. This is especially true of actions that may become absorbed in the ordinary conduct of a treatment.

The Reality Question and Its Treatment

In an excellent review of the psychoanalytic literature on the manner in which some patients, primarily those with perverse behavior, distort reality, Grossman (1993) adds his own voice to a number of analysts who seem vexed with this problem. Just as T. S. Eliot is quoted as saying, "Human kind cannot bear very much reality" (James, 1998), so a host of writers bear witness to a sort of joint effort to remedy deficient reality testing among this group of patients. Most of the combined literature starts with Freud's work on fetishism (Freud, 1927) and proceeds to Arlow's claim that a blurring of reality involves an interposition of a fantasy fetish (Arlow, 1971). Renik (1992) attempts to clarify the distinctions among psychoses, neuroses, and fetishism in the construction of reality. He begins by describing a time that a psychotic woman accused him of yelling at her when she was twenty minutes late for a session, and he claims to explain this alteration of reality by attributing projection and externalization to her. It may be fair, however, to wonder if this woman also perceived Renik's anger at her for being late. If that is possible, one can begin to examine what other issues were alive in the study of a patient's misperceptions. This is not meant to be a post hoc form of supervision, but rather a suggestion for consideration. Once again, only by giving credence to the patient's anger are we able to capture the sector that is not acknowledged.

This attention to just one part of the split is beautifully taken up in Grossman's (1993) tale of a patient who adamantly refused to acknowledge that his analysis was nearing an end, inasmuch as he was being forced to move to another town. Grossman, after a prolonged period of patience, writes: "Finally, the analyst told the patient that it was clear that they would not be able to continue past a certain date, and that he needed to make plans accordingly." Now there is some slight ambiguity in that sentence as to whether the plans had to be made by the patient or the analyst. But it seems not to matter, because each of these persons had to make plans and so, once again, we wonder whether something about the analyst is contributing to the supposed failure to perceive and act on reality. The explanation that is ordinarily offered insists that the patient needs to have the reality pointed out. But perhaps, just as with the psychotic woman, the patient is aware of the real world and, in this instance, knows that the analyst needs this statement as much for himself as for the patient. This possibility once again refocuses our own perception on what may be happening to the analyst, and once again mutual enactment seems to prevail.

This new version of the confusion of tongues is brought to even greater clarity as Renik (1992) describes the necessity of having to force a termination to bring home reality to a patient. Although his reasons are clear, they are less than convincing. They center on the patient's preferring to use the analyst—according to Renik—as a fetish, rather than *looking at* how she uses him. That is to say that the analyst feels that she merged with him as an idealized and omnipotent source of capacities that she lacked, and so she hoped analysis would last forever. Although Renik claims that he as analyst is not a privileged interpreter of reality, he seems to contradict this view by insisting on termination as a solution to this dilemma. There can be no working through of an idealized merger with an analyst who, while discouraging a full-blown idealization, simultaneously disavows his own reality. This is certainly not meant to say that this turn of events would or could markedly change the course of this analysis; rather, my point is to highlight the mutual split between the patient and the analyst. Thus one must add to mutual enactment this phenomenon of a reciprocal configuration.

Forced termination for a patient with an idealizing selfobject transference, rather than being a working-through, is tantamount to a traumatic deidealization. It will necessarily lead to depression, even if the analysis is subsequently recast as successful. It is probably akin to what was previously discussed as a suppression of one sector in a vertical split: It does seem to be effective in resolving or ending the treatment in some cases, but effectiveness is no reliable guide to correctness.

Grossman (1993) continues the theme of the troubling problem of reality with an emphasis on the role of the superego and the role of the analyst as the advocate of giving reality its due. One cannot make any certain judgment about Grossman's case vignette about a patient who felt that he had reported a dream to his analyst despite the fact that he had not come to his hour because of an accident. The analyst reminded the patient of this miss, and reported to the reader the analytic material that followed his intervention. This is intriguing, but the reader cannot help but be puzzled as to just what *that* miss meant to the analyst. Although we are told that the patient did indeed keep the missed hour in mind, we are not privy to its place in the mind of the analyst. Our wonder is open to imaginings about how the analyst sees himself, if, as he claims is true, he sees his patient as "away from the center of awareness" (p. 431). All of this material sees the analyst as an objective judge of reality. Rather than abandoning such objectivity and allying oneself solely with the patient's subjectivity, however, it is probable that both are necessary. Most therapists seem to accomplish this integration, but they resist noting the elements of reciprocal subjectivity. The split of the patient meets a corresponding split in the therapist. Each sees reality objectively and subjectively. The analyst may have a more intact superego, but this supposed moral superiority is a state of affairs that cannot be imposed on the patient.

The Dual Transference

Seeing the role of an analyst as one of presenting patients with "the nonsensical and self-destructive results of their contradictory attitude" (Reed, 1997, p. 1177) in order to make their "subsequent presentation of hostility and envy more tolerable to them and therefore more possible" sets a tone of opposition between patient and analyst. Not surprisingly, this stance manages to create and subsequently find enormous anger in patients, and it usually permits reactive retaliation by therapists. It *is* surprising, however, that the "years spent" (p. 1176) in these pursuits are not examined as open to reconsideration. It is not necessarily the case that a patient's use of the analyst, or the analysis, or the interpretations of the analyst is equivalent to a perversion, as suggested by these authors. Rather, this use of the analyst is a manifestation of a structural deficit, because, like it or not, that is what a split represents. The selfobject relationship is missing and thus it is needed to heal the split, and no amount of "uncovering vengefulness" (p. 1176) will do the trick. It is important to note that sometimes one sector of the split is enacted outside of the treatment yet remains a transference, whereas sometimes both sectors are involved in the treatment as transferences, one exhibiting a "realistic stance" compared with the other. Following is a typical example.

Case Illustration

A physician in analysis had a long history of sexual acting-out with female patients. This behavior consisted of elaborate physical examinations in which he manipulated them to perform fellatio on him. Much of this behavior had subsided during his analysis, but one day he reported a recurrence. He was shame-faced and embarrassed to speak of it, but it could be fairly accurately placed as following a wish of his for a change in his analytic appointment time. He found it impossible to ask for this change. The reluctance was a familiar one traceable to his being sternly chastened during his childhood for waking his mother during the night with his severe recurrent leg pain. He feared being a bother to her, because she became quite upset over being awakened. The pain was later diagnosed as a smoldering osteomyelitis, but his memory was fixed on his bearing of the pain and not complaining. This state of silent suffering existed for many years. He grew to be a taciturn individual who bore his difficulties without complaints, and throughout his life until adulthood felt pride in this accomplishment. His childhood of suffering was the telescoped memory of this particular forced silence of his anguish, which became the focus of an entire life of not asking and not complaining. As he recounted the details of his recent aberrant sexual behavior, it became clear that the entire episode had had to be conducted entirely in silence with no hint of his asking for the cooperation of his female patients. What seemed to be an almost pantomime performance of sexual activity also seemed to characterize his own need to conceal his personal wishes. This patient's difficulties in his practice surfaced after a number of such episodes, but in treatment he began to see a diminution and finally a disappearance of their occurrences. It is often the case that acting-out behavior subsides in treatment, and then over time becomes a part of the treatment as it is transformed into an acting-in, either in the telling or the overt behavior.

The clear message of this patient's acting without asking could be read within the treatment by way of his longing for a changed appointment without being able to make an overt request. As an aside here, it is extremely important that the therapist recognize that the schedule of the hours offers the patient something in the way of a structural framework, which becomes a form of his very psychological structure and integrity. Thus the regularity of the treatment now stands for one essential meaning of the treatment. To concern ourselves with a preoccupation about the patient grasping the content of an interpretation may well lead one astray from the more correct need to understand the particular form or configuration of the treatment. Missing hours are more properly recognized as denoting missing psychological structure than as masking one or more favored fantasies about what the miss as content might mean. Thus the wish for a changed appointment has ramifications that must be first realized in the patient's need to regularize his life.

If the therapist is able to see both the need for the hour along with the need of the patient not to make a request, the two can be brought together in the form and content of an interpretation. This patient's particular history allowed me to make an interpretation along with a genetic reconstruction. This is only a total and integrated interpretation if I, as therapist, am able to comprehend how *I* felt about the request and the irregularity. I had to recognize how much I needed to see him, and how much of a burden he was. I needed to empathize not only with him but with his mother as well. We must not forget that this patient saw his mother's inability to relieve his pain along with her silent plea for his silence. His uncanny ability to choose compliant female patients for his sexual exploits seemed to give testimony to his perception of the willing muteness of the other. Of course, the therapist can claim a compliant ignorance in that there may have been no way of guessing at the wish of the patient that preceded the activity with the compliant woman patient. Seen as a transference configuration, the therapist is *both* the mother who is deaf to the needs of her child and also is the parent who holds out the standards of proper behavior. This dual role operates in all of the case reports of frustrated analysts who insist that their patients have corrupt superegos or aim to debase or devalue the analyst. Only when the duality is brought together in the person of the analyst is a reciprocal union leading to healing possible for the patient.

It is certainly difficult for therapists intent on exposing the "sexual and aggressive" drives of their patients to move to a the-

ory in which they visualize themselves as selfobjects who function
as psychological structures for their patients. Once this change in
perspective is achieved, however, one is able to ascertain the needs
of the patient who asks for particular narcissistic sustenance.
Elsewhere the careful delineation and description of the working
through of these transferences has been made available (Kohut,
1971) and so will not be repeated here. What needs to be under-
lined is that the parallel sectors of the vertical split require
responses that may or may not be similar. The sectors are both
separate and distinct. My physician patient took a great deal of
pride in his mute acceptance of adversity, and one may readily see
as much in his proud presentation of his erect penis to an equally
silent and submissive subject. This can be read as a grandiose and
exhibitionist display that is a primitive expression of, and a sexualization of, his narcissistic self-state. Parallel to this display, the
equally necessary wish to be heard and responded to can be seen
as his wish to be cared for and to have his pain lessened by an
idealized other. This sector is not necessarily one that is fueled by
a grandiose fantasy, but rather one asking for nurturing. It may
initially be seen as stating that "I need nothing and so ask for
nothing." That initially contrasts the asking versus not asking.
The analyst must recognize and match—in understanding but not
in action—these parallel sectors. As the patient asks of his analyst
these two requests: "look at and admire me" along with "look
after and take care of me," it is vitally important that they be
brought together, so that he can ultimately feel both looked after
and admired. Each request is experienced differently by the analyst, and each can be a source of burden or willing compliance.
Only with this union will the split sectors be brought into an integrated whole. It should not need to be said, but perhaps it will
not hurt to emphasize, that here one need only interpret. The
folly of feeling one must respond in kind to these transference
presentations is probably at the same level as that of missing their
meaning and noting only the predictable rage that follows such
neglect. Interpretation lies happily between gratification and mis-
taken insistence.

There are therefore two ways in which the dual transference
fails to be established and worked through to an integrated
whole. The first may occur more often in a psychotherapy in
which the patient is seen only once or twice weekly. It need not be
true of all such cases, however. The crucial factor is the position

of the therapist who chooses to concentrate on a single sector and not allow the development of a corresponding split in himself. This was probably the case of the psychiatrist in chapter 8 who treated the unfaithful husband who was urged to "get back on the horse." This case corresponds to a supportive treatment wherein one sector is supported and strengthened by an alliance with the therapist.

The second type of failure to engage and work through the dual transference occurs in treatments that are frequent and intensive enough to encourage the transference but in which, unfortunately, the therapist may be unable to appreciate it. Here we find instances of allegiance to a theory that serves more as a straitjacket than an enabling device. There are, however, a number of such treatments that proceed to success by way of an identification with the therapist that, over time, does dominate and integrate the split.

When we earlier discussed the form of disavowal seen in those patients who are overwhelmed by anxiety or depression rather than exhibiting personality or behavior disorders, we noted that the collusion of the parents did not allow these patients to perceive the world accurately. The cases of Fritz and Larry were those of individuals periodically seized by dysphoric affects that were never fully integrated into their personalities. The issue of identification was noted in that discussion and was touched on later in our study of the superego, its contents, and idealization. Patients who cannot allow themselves to misbehave or exhibit traits of a narcissistic personality disorder are those whose superego in each sector is too stern to allow any sort of self-indulgent or self-aggrandizing organization. The split-off sector is thus usually characterized by anxiety, and its contents are not allowed into direct consciousness. They are not repressed, however, inasmuch as that defensive maneuver would lead to a successful banishment, whereas disavowal allows the periodic return and recognition of these unacknowledged perceptions.

In the treatment of these conditions, the therapist becomes the vehicle of integration to the extent that he or she can observe and tolerate the content of the disavowed material. These areas of separated and unrecognized issues become available to scrutiny and reveal themselves as emotional but not behavioral sets that are felt to be unbearable. They may be felt to be unbearable by the therapist as well. Fritz, for example, had intense anxiety that translated into equally intense rage and disappointment at an impotent father. He felt that it was impossible for him ever to be open with this anger for fear of a further loss. In this particular instance, the elucidation of the dynamics took place outside of the transference in relation to other significant figures in Fritz's life, and the therapist was used primarily to validate Fritz's perceptions and feelings. A similar course of therapy proved effective for Larry, who likewise worked out a complex set of dependency needs outside of the transference. The basic point for consideration in the emergence of an emotional state with psychological content, as opposed to mere panic or other dysphoric states, hinges on the patient's perception of the therapist's capacity to encourage and endure its overt exposure. Larry initially had a therapist who tended to tease and taunt any indication of childishness or hint of demandingness. This therapist felt that Larry had to act more grown-up and "get over" acting like a baby. Inasmuch as Larry partly agreed with this appraisal of this segregated part, there developed a union of suppression between patient and therapist. These perceptions of patients determine the ultimate fate of dissociated aspects of the personality and thus lead to the crucial problem of the corresponding split in the therapist, which can certainly be seen as a unique form of countertransference.

The Split in the Therapist

The ideal course of treatment of patients with a vertical split ultimately involves a matching or reciprocal division in the therapist. This division immediately presents a number of challenges and questions. Is this split potentially available in all therapists and, if so, how is it accessed? Is this split a matter of a proper match between a certain patient and a therapist with a similar problem? Does a patient have to find such a potential, if unspoken, connection to get better, and is this a powerful component to the studies on such matches (Kantrowitz, 1996)? Perhaps even more important, can a patient avoid the pain of therapeutic work by way of an alliance with a therapist who covertly or even openly tolerates a similar sort of behavior? Whether one may choose to consider this as a certain variation of countertransference, it seems clear that to claim it as either necessary or inevitable or both opens up a new set of parameters for the treatment. These new parameters vary from the therapist who remains blind to the split by a dogged allegiance to one side of the separation, on to one who openly embraces the opposing side. Interestingly, each seems guided by a certain morality that ranges from doing what is right and proper to doing what is a full and complete expression of one's self and one's potentialities. In the struggle against a recognition of one's own split, rationalization becomes extremely useful.

If we recall the case illustration of the unfaithful husband whose first therapist subtly condoned infidelity, we see one form of a match that is detrimental to the ultimate recovery of the patient. Yet another case would demonstrate that a patient will run through a whole series of therapists, until he or she finds one that properly fits. This was seen in the case of a patient who wanted his therapist to sign a form supporting his disability. Only a therapist who was able to join in this corruption could possibly help this patient, but this corruption needed to become the central point of the treatment to enable the patient to integrate his own disavowed sector. Therapists rather uniformly claim to be principled and realistic, so the questions raised rarely involve whether to treat a patient. Do we send corrupt or delinquent patients to like-minded therapists or to models of morality? If we feel strongly about a certain form of behavior, are we more likely to help or to hinder the patient's recovery?

To answer our questions in order, we begin with the claim that supports the potential availability of a concordant split in all therapists. Putting all the caveats to the side for the moment, this availability probably requires no more than the usual empathic listening posture, with the addition of an alertness to an alteration or reappearance of one sector or another. If one looks at behavior disorders as our most illustrative example, one must be able to understand each sector as it presents itself. The misbehaving physician must induce the same trial identification as the image of the good doctor. The patient who misses an appointment and forgets that he has missed it needs to be helped to discover what that missed appointment may mean to him; merely pointing it out may not be necessary or even helpful. The very fact of the existence of the corresponding split is of enormous help to the therapist in his or her understanding. Here countertransference is very much a part of ignorance, and as one's interest in accessing the split-off part is enhanced, it becomes more and more available. Perhaps the best clue to one's personal blindness is the feeling of frustration that is so common in our literature, and that often is accompanied by a plea to offer a new theoretical embellishment that will support the therapist's expression of exasperation.

The next question about the match between patient and therapist has some fascinating ramifications, because clinical experience allows opposing answers. It comes down to some patients needing a therapist—especially in behavior disorders—who is familiar with a particular set of feelings; some other patients would run a risk with this same type of therapist. To achieve a trial identification with an unfaithful husband, one must be able to live freely with that fantasy, but one cannot live it out with a patient. We seek a delicate balance in that we need to get close enough to know and struggle with a feeling that might ordinarily be readily banished. If we quickly embrace a righteous stance, we may tip the balance and fail to serve our patient.

The next move is to an equally dangerous position espoused by those who embrace what is called "healthy pornography, healthy sadomasochism, healthy non-monogamy" (Verghese, 1998), and thereby take an equally moral and nontherapeutic stance. One may not be able to avoid a judgmental position, but it must be seen as secondary to an effort to unravel the overall meaning to a patient. Patients do not suffer from "healthy sadomasochism," nor are they helped by a judgment that may encourage that strange combination of words. Rather, our suffering patients are often also sadomasochistic, which needs neither to be condemned nor to be condoned, or at least that judgment can be postponed until it is understood.

For a proper match between patient and therapist, the issue of the vertical split is often one of the most interesting to study. Patients who suffer from behavior disorders often do a great deal of shopping in their effort to find a proper therapist. They also tend to leave rather quickly if the balance they seek in a therapist is disturbed. Patients with personality disorders seem less likely to be sensitive to each sector being recognized, whereas patients with dysphoric, dissociated states are most content with a therapist who is relatively oblivious to their disavowed material. A similar lack of recognition can also occur when a behavior disorder is not allowed to enter the treatment.

The aim of all of the varied treatments is facilitating the union of the split. This integration is achieved by way of the split transference being joined together in the person of the therapist and so conveying this understanding of the union to the patient. The physician patient who acted out outside of the treatment is soon able to experience the duality of his relationship to the therapist within the treatment. The child who cannot ask joins with the one who needs. He needs both admiration and nurturing. No doubt in many persons this is a mere expression of ambivalence, and the same can be said of a therapist who feels both a wish to care for a patient and a wish to be rid of that same patient. It is different in cases of a vertical split, because the sectors do not appear either at the same time or in the same place. This, then, is the problem that must be surmounted to achieve an integration, and this is done entirely by interpretations that connect both in depth and across the split. No doubt a host of therapists have over the years been effective without offering the kind of interpretation that is suggested here. The natural course of our own history of therapy reveals many clinical experiences that defy our explanatory efforts.

Inasmuch as the origin of the split lies in a collusion with a parent who does not allow some aspect of reality to be acknowledged, the same unverbalized material is very likely to be realized in treatment. The therapist becomes involved in an enacted replay of the childhood, and one may conceptualize this replay with a variety of theoretical concepts that range from projected identification to psychological merger. The resulting circumstances are best seen as the therapist being induced into a connection with the split-off sector. The work that is required of the therapist involves a personal awareness of his own split, an effort to join with it in the form of a personal integration of his own, and then an interpretive effort at working it through with his or her patient.

Case Illustration

Kenneth, an analytic candidate well along in his training, came to see his supervisor in a troubled state because he had twice fallen asleep while his patient lay silent on the analytic couch. Kenneth felt especially upset, because it was unusual that he fall asleep with a patient, and this unfortunate occurrence was, for Kenneth, one of the worst things that could befall his patient. His patient spent a good deal of his time on the couch without speaking and would later explain to his analyst that he was unable to talk because of the intensity of his feelings. He was not willfully silent; rather, he had to process some of his fantasies and emotions in order to talk about them—or so he said. The time spent in silent thought was a time apart from his analyst, in which the patient had strong but unutterable emotions. Kenneth had devised a number of exercises to occupy himself until his patient felt ready and able to speak; at times he busied himself with crossword puzzles.

Kenneth's patient was raised by an alcoholic mother who was often preoccupied. Only later in the patient's adulthood was this state of the mother's emotional absence explained by the diagnosis of alcoholism. The patient recalled an intense relief on finally being able to understand just why his mother could not attend to him. One startling example of the mother's inattention was the story of the patient being left at a large department store with the mother leaving by herself. The panicky return of the mother to the store to reclaim her forgotten child was etched in the patient's memory.

When Kenneth was awakened from his sleep by the patient calling out his name, he felt chagrined and bewildered. He told his supervisor that he felt as if he had been chosen by some secret diabolical process to relive this patient's childhood trauma. He then reported attending a clinical conference during which a teacher had told the budding analysts that patients who did not conform to the basic rule of free association were to be considered unanalyzable and dismissed. Kenneth was aghast at this suggestion but wondered if it applied to his silent patient, who was certainly not doing what was required of a patient. He reported to his supervisor that he had been feeling unusually free and unburdened this past week, and his own analyst had suggested to Kenneth that he had been inviting punishment to undo this newfound sense of well-being.

As a start one can certainly see the entire episode as centered on Kenneth's psychology with little or nothing to do with the patient. This focus treats this enactment as a failure of the analyst, and it was supported by Kenneth's fantasy of being bawled out by his supervisor, because he had earlier told Kenneth to stop doing something else felt to be deleterious to the patient. If we move to a consideration of the enactment as mutual participation, we can see a split of the patient into the silent and the verbal

parts, and a corresponding split of the analyst. If one next con-
jures up an image of the abandoned child in the department store,
it may be possible to be empathic with the mother who alter-
nately disregards the child and then rescues him in panic. To
recast the analyst in this dual role of neglect and concern, sleep
and wakefulness, preoccupation and attention is to see the correspondingly dual message of the patient. This reciprocal relationship demands that the patient's division into being ignored and
being helped is underscored by a communication that may read
as follows: "I am self sufficient and need no one" along with "I
am not to be ignored and must be looked after."

If the analyst is to realize the transference with this patient, it
may, or perhaps must, be done so in the form of a mutual enactment. The supervisor suggested that the patient had lulled the
analyst to sleep by the nonverbal message that said he needed no
one. That is what a burdened mother and a burdened analyst
wish to hear (i.e., "I am now free of this child"). This message is
followed and joined by the parallel sector, which wakens the analyst and mother from private reverie with a loud demand for
attention that underscores the failing of the analyst as mother.
There is no doubt that this process interdigitates with the readiness of the analyst to be so engaged, but we once again wonder if
a successful treatment requires that some of these transferences be
actualized in behavior.

To be sure, this may be but a very minor gloss on the thesis that
everything that takes place in treatment is an interaction (Goldberg,
1995). Whether the relationship is discussed as interpersonal or
intersubjective or self-selfobject, there is a consensus about the
essence of this mutual construction. *What is emphasized in the
study of the vertical split is the divided mutuality plus, in the behavior disorders, the overt action seen in one sector.*

One cannot generalize as to the range of emotional reactions
that a therapist will have to the communicative system that
emerges between these two initially silent systems. It is always
seen as more dramatic in behavior disorders, and one is well
advised to be especially alert in these matters. A patient who pro-
poses special arrangements in either the schedule or the fee may
be attempting to set up a split-off enactment. These proposals are
not to be seen as efforts to "get away with something," and certainly should not be condemned out of hand by resorting to a set
of standard rules and regulations. The issue is less one of propri-

ety than of the need of the split-off sector to find a place for itself. It must be able to emerge and then be examined as opposed to an immediate suppression under the guise of correctness. There is a natural reluctance to tolerate being uncomfortable with patients who are unwilling or unable to become "good patients" in their ability to conform. This reluctance now must be highlighted as a signal of a wish to engage a split silently. Perhaps most important, it must be recognized that the segregated material must somehow make itself known to the therapist if it is ever to be understood and its effects diminished.

The Underlying Depression

Split-off material has its own unique regulatory purpose that allows the parallel or dominating sector to function properly and be relatively free of painful affects. The fantasies and character of patients with personality disorders handle the narcissistic injuries of everyday life by a psychological effort that restores equilibrium. The dissociated material of patients with panic attacks and other episodic dysphoric experiences enables a large percentage of their lives to be free of anxiety. Behavior disorders restore psychic equilibrium and obliterate painful affect states. Thus it is a truism that any and all efforts to remove or alter these workable defenses will increase the discomfort that is the reason for their very existence.

As the therapist assumes an active and meaningful transference position, the previously-noted solution, as fragile and unsuccessful as it may be, now shifts to the relationship of replacement (i.e., to the therapist). Ordinarily, what is seen first as a diminution of symptoms, along with an increased reliance on the treatment, is followed by a reappearance of the symptoms that have now become part of the therapeutic conversation. As this becomes a center of concern, the symptom is seen as unreliable, and soon it begins to erode. In a significant majority of cases this erosion exposes an underlying depression of a rather specific type. This depression is not one of guilt or superego condemnation but rather consists of emptiness and purposelessness. A few of these patients will be familiar with this unpleasant affect, but for many it is totally new and equally surprising. One would guess that a certain small degree of this negative affect had regularly reared its head only to be quickly dispelled by disavowal and active behavior.

The specific treatment of this depression runs a range of possibilities from more intensive therapy to pharmacological intervention. It is very likely that the changes in brain chemistry that occur with many of the aberrant behaviors are tantamount to a form of self-medication akin to the output of those endorphins that lead to feelings of elation. For some patients, especially those with behavior disorders associated with addictive qualities, hospitalization should be considered. No one gives up a split-off sector without a penalty or a price. One does need to recognize that some of the major work of the treatment takes place in these periods of depression. Some therapists experience increased discomfort here; others are relieved to see the suffering that has been concealed for so long a time. The specific form of the therapeutic work has to do with a nontraumatic relinquishment of the therapeutic relationship that is best conceptualized as a selfobject transference. That process is well described elsewhere (Kohut, 1971), and I have also indicated that no specific set of dynamics can be regularly expected (Goldberg, 1995). Therefore one cannot detail a predictable sequence of therapeutic interventions. To be sure, the usual dynamics correlated with depression, that is, the action of a hostile superego venting itself on the ego, ordinarily do not apply. Though persons with behavior disorders may be guilty and persons with personality disorders may be filled with shame, the depression that is inevitably unearthed is not one of guilt or shame. The therapeutic handling of the depression depends on interpretive work that deals with the underlying set of fantasies and the phase-specific relinquishment of the selfobjects.

Can one attribute any particular set of dynamic or familiar conflict features to the vertical split? The range of severity of the problem makes it very unlikely, except for what may be the most general sort of echo of what Kohut characterized as "tragic man," that is, someone who is unable to fulfill a life plan, whose energies are consumed by pathological structures, and who thereby cannot confront the world in its entirety.

The Integrative Interpretation

Ordinarily in thinking of repression or the horizontal split, one visualizes interpretation as working from the top downward (i.e., vertically). The repressed or hidden material is allowed to come to the surface (i.e., once again vertically). In contrast with the up-down arrow of the interpretive work in the undoing of repression, the arrow for the healing of the vertical split is best pictured as going from side to side. The main direction in repression is downward as interpretation aims for the unconscious. The main direction in disavowal is from the reality ego toward the split-off segment and is usually pictured as going from right to left. Just as the goal in undoing repression is to make conscious the unconscious, so too is the goal in dealing with the vertical split to make a place for it in the reality sector. They both involve some illustration of union or integration.

It is generally agreed that disavowal is regularly joined with repression (Laplanche and Pontalis, 1967), and so a superficial connection of the parallel sectors is never sufficient for integration. Telling my physician patient that he acts out when anxious is but a preliminary step to the in-depth interpretive work that is needed. Once again, there is a need to recognize that the sectors are at odds with each other on the surface, but one cannot make a claim that the same is true of them unconsciously. Here is another example of the split and how it may be dealt with in one instance.

Pathological Lying

Eric, the patient introduced earlier (chapter 5), entered psychoanalysis for a multitude of characterological problems having to do with marital troubles, lack of friends, and subjective feelings of depression. He had had many previous efforts at treatment, and at least one of them was characterized by a long period of what must be termed brutalization by a therapist who screamed at and belittled him. In retrospect it seemed to be the case that this therapist's professed aim was to keep the patient "in his place," and much of the outlandish behavior of the therapist had to do with the emergence of the patient's grandiosity, which probably threatened this therapist. Here is another example of an enactment involving a split in the therapist.

One day Eric told of applying for a new and favored position in a company and therefore of his feeling it necessary that he concoct a false resume concerning his education. Although this was not the first instance of his lying behavior, it was striking in that it was difficult to see the need for it. Eric launched into a detailed story of how the lie was indeed needed to ensure his application, and this was coupled with the unlikelihood of his ever being exposed as lying. Without the lie he would be seen as less of a person, and so the lie was more than justified because "these people" would otherwise not hire him. He insisted that this necessary lie troubled him not a whit and even allowed him a certain comfort in his anticipation of a new and better position.

As I puzzled over the nature of this bit of misbehavior, I also struggled with a feeling directed toward cautioning Eric about the folly of his lying, of instructing him about the "right" way to behave, and even of chastising him for this outrageous example of excess. My own uncertainty allowed the time for some of these same thoughts to come from my patient without my voicing them.

Either from an identification with his agitated previous therapist or perhaps originating from another aspect of himself, Eric soon confessed his own problems with his having lied. He would never be able to feel he had rightfully gained the job. There may have been no need to have made up this fictional resume. There would always be a shadow over his achievement of this position. He might even get caught. But the other voice would also rise in opposition insisting that it was the right thing, and he had no cause for doubt. The battle seemed equally joined, but shortly after this incident the patient reported that he discovered himself lying in a situation in which there was no possible reason or justification. Indeed, he was somewhat startled to hear this lie issue forth from his lips, because it was so clearly of no value to himself or anyone. He, for one, felt critical of seeming to be what he clearly felt he was not—or was he? He was so at odds with himself that he was unable to feel sure about just what position he would most likely embrace. At this point he felt allied with being honest and aboveboard, but he well knew how the fraudulent personality could present itself with equal vigor and an equal sense of certainty and justification.

The analytic work with this patient had mainly to do with the gradual emergence of his grandiosity, which initially seemed hardly hidden at all in his pathological lying. That grandiosity clearly revealed itself in the lies, but the particulars of the fantasy, involving taking over the entire company, soon made the lies seem lightweight. The further work on the nature of the unexpressed grandiosity was an interesting exercise in its relation to the sector of the personality that was initially seen as reasonable and critical. As the excitement of confronting deeper grandiose fantasies was confronted, there was a corresponding increase in the intensity of the critical agency. One could, of course, see this phenomenon as the presence of a harsh superego over the potentially emerging unconscious impulses, but the peculiarly different character of this process was the side-by-side conscious comparison that became available and clear to each of us. For instance, the grandiose fantasy of becoming president of the company was accompanied by one in which he felt that his coworkers were allied together in a conspiratorial effort to defeat his progress. To be sure, both lay claim to grandiosity, and therefore probably derived from a more unitary and outrageous megalomanic form of ideation. This potentially common origin—which was later confirmed—became the vehicle of our interpretive work. The first order of business, however, was to deal with the split by focusing on the long-range need for integration, achieved by interpreting both sides in sequence or in tandem. Thus, this particular patient might have his fantasies interpreted in what follows in a simplified form.

1. In the transference—"You are very excited about applying for the job and you feel that I am very proud of you. You also feel that I will get all the credit for what you have done—or that I want now to be rid of you. You are equally critical of yourself. You feel your accomplishments in life will be ignored by me, or else I will take the credit for them." The therapist is asked to mirror the patient, and the therapist is simultaneously asked to squelch the patient.
2. Outside the transference—"Your feeling about achieving prominence in the company is so exciting that you dampen it by feeling there is a network of conspiracy against you."
3. The patient feels that no mirroring is available, and so must struggle to suppress the excitement of his fantasies. If this sector becomes a part of the transference, it may begin by lying to the therapist but will ultimately join in an integrated grandiosity. In reconstructing the past—"Your mother dressed you to be the handsomest boy in the class, while your father argued with her over showing you off. You did not know whether to be proud or humble."

Beneath all these statements is the overexciting fantasy akin to winning the Nobel Prize or curing the family unhappiness or other familiar issues of greatness. The integrative interpretation cannot be limited to one side or the other: not to education or to empathy alone, but to both (see chapter 11).

As the capacity of the patient to see the connection between the splits increased, both the pathological lying and its critical counterpart decreased. Integration or unification of the split does strengthen and help reorganize the self. The unified self allows the grandiosity to be tamed or handled much as a single faucet allows the mix of very hot and very cold water to emerge at a warm and tolerable temperature.

In summary, patients with vertical splits can be enabled to recreate the split in treatment by way of a dual or parallel transference. This duality must be met by an appropriate role in the therapist. The joining together of the divided psyche is achieved by interpretations that move both vertically to unconscious material and horizontally to disavowed sectors. The final aim of the treatment is an integrated self.

Chapter 10

VARIETIES OF THE SPLIT

It may be possible to organize a certain continuum of types of pathology that manifest the vertical split. At one end are cases such as Fritz and Larry whose symptoms betray a segregated parallel self filled with negative affect, and so are to be avoided and feared. This pathology is often considered to represent a dissociated state. That term is probably less than helpful, however, because it is also applied to the dissociation attributed to multiple personality disorders, where there is said to lurk elaborate displays of several or even many other selves. The controversy over whether the last category represents a bona fide type of psychopathology will not be resolved here, save to note how many persons claim that its existence depends on the prejudices of the investigator (Spanos, 1996). If such a set of disorders does exist, these patients would be placed at the opposite pole from those cases with a more limited eruption of dysphoric states (e.g., Fritz and Larry). This placement would seem to be in keeping with the stories of extreme abuse suffered by persons with multiple personality disorder during childhood, and so they would be expected to manifest the most severe forms of pathology (Bremner and Marmar, 1998). The two extremes of these disorders each shows a self or selves divided.

The planned diagnostic handbook would probably place the narcissistic personality disorders in the next least serious position, inasmuch as they show a division that maintains its pathology in

the realm of fantasies or character. The narcissistic behavior disorders would then follow as being more serious or pathological.
Thus one may be able to posit such a linear series and support it
with a linkage to the basic psychological structure and some general developmental issues. The background thesis would be that
sicker patients have the more fragile and disorganized structures,
that the split is more pronounced and perhaps even multiple, and
that it is correlated with a significant degree of childhood pathology. The healthier patients would tend toward less severe developmental difficulties. Thus we have a series from a limited split
to a significant one to the most severe form, the controversial
multiple personality disorders.

To consider the possibility of such a linear series, we can follow the fate of a succession of typical cases that show a similar
problem in psychodynamics but clearly evidence different degrees
and kinds of pathology.

Case 1—A Limited and Circumscribed Dissociation

Jerome is a young man who developed attacks of anxiety diagnosed as panic attacks by a psychiatrist, who thereupon placed
him on medication. He gained only moderate relief from this
treatment regimen and was referred for psychotherapy. Jerome
told a story of these attacks first occurring as if "out of the blue"
while he was riding in a car with his parents. The panic became
so severe that they had to pull off the road, and the father gave
Jerome a Xanax that he had saved from a prescription given him
some time ago by an internist. This brought some immediate
relief, and Jerome eagerly hoped that a medication selected just
for him and prescribed by a psychiatrist would help him even
more. The Xanax turned out to be of only temporary assistance,
however, and the succession of medications offered by the new
prescriber seemed to run out of effectiveness over time. He was
discouraged because, in his own words, he felt that he had lost
control of his life.

The history that was told to the new therapist was of a fairly
contented young man of age 20 who was just finishing high
school and making plans to go off to college. He had an older
brother who was now about to finish his own college education.
He was shocked recently to learn that the money that his parents

had set aside for college for both his brother and himself had been exhausted for the brother's education. His parents said that they had miscalculated, and that he would have to take out a loan for his own education. Much to his dismay, they also told him that he would have to pay back this loan on his own. The parents had never informed either of their children about their financial miscalculation and confessed that they had been privately very worried about this inevitable day of reckoning. Jerome's panic attacks began shortly after he learned of his plight. Neither he nor his parents were able to connect these two facts.

During Jerome's psychotherapy what emerged was not his fearfulness at having to fend for himself but rather the intense rage at his parents for concealing both their financial predicament and its unfortunate results from him. He had never before been at all consciously aware of just how angry he was at his parents, but as he came more in possession of this knowledge it came to the forefront. And with this possession there followed first a diminution and then a disappearance of the panic attacks. Jerome later likened this knowledge (i.e., of how he saw and felt about the situation) to the sort of feeling of control that the first Xanax had given him. Just as the chemical disarray that led to his panic attacks was outside of his awareness and control, so too was the unconscious hostility that he lived with; it resided in an area inaccessible to him.

During the psychotherapy Jerome became more and more aware of his feelings toward his parents, and he examined these feelings against a backdrop of whether they were reasonable and legitimate. It was one thing to be mad at his parents for what they had done, but it was another thing to ascertain that his anger was justified. As the area of perceived anger was confronted and then enlarged on, Jerome became genuinely befuddled as to his right to be so angry. This particular state of cloudiness that is frequently noted in the treatment of patients with a vertical split is best seen as an intermediary point in these patients' ability to perceive a reality that will be tolerable to them. All of the ingredients of superego and ego ideal content came to bear as Jerome struggled with what was clearly felt as a betrayal by one or both parents. It is not uncommon for a therapist to claim a very clear and even obvious point of view as to the justification of, for example, rage or disappointment, whereas the patient correspondingly feels at a loss as to his rightful ownership of these feelings. One naturally tends merely to explain or show by example to the patient how one should correctly assess a situation, but it is essential that the patient be able to work through these feelings of betrayal. Sometimes patients sheepishly say that they feel foolish in not knowing what is right or wrong, and they turn to the therapist for guidance. Rather than undertaking an effort at education, one should recognize that the patient *also* knows what is right; this is the vertical split in operation.

In this case vignette we see the implicit parental demand for some aspect of reality to be ignored or at least not to be psychologically reckoned with by either themselves or their son. Inasmuch as the latter now has to live with a set of negative feelings, to wit, his intense rage at his parents, he is called on to put this to the side somehow in the manner of an act of "sublation," to use one proposed term as noted in chapter 3. This struggle resolved by this mechanism is best understood as one of disillusionment with the parental ego ideal, which is now seen as unreliable. The material of resentment is not repressed or suppressed but rather lives on in a different place. When it is accessed, it makes for a different person. This seems to be a reasonable start for considering a parallel sector that has a different reality along with different ambitions and goals. To be sure, it is initially experienced by the remainder of the personality as offensive but, over time, it is generally able to be integrated into the totality of the self.

Case 2—Narcissistic Personality Disorder

With this next case, we advance both the extent and the severity of the vertical split. Aaron is a middle-aged lawyer who is readily characterized by almost everyone whom he meets as both charming and obnoxious. He is charming in situations where he feels comfortable, in control, and wishing to win someone over. He is obnoxious in the context of losing control, not getting his way, and wishing to make someone behave in some particular manner. He is charming when he is with an important client to whom he can be unbelievably sensitive, focused, and helpful. Aaron has thus gained a reputation for competence, efficiency, and even personal concern. He is quickly moved to an imperious and insensitive demeanor, however, if he feels ignored or insulted.

Aaron came into treatment because of marital problems, but

rather soon admitted to lifelong feelings of agitation and worry. He is the second son of a father who was also an attorney and died when the patient was in his teens. His mother is described in such a casual manner that it borders on the dismissive. Aaron says that she was and is primarily involved with his older sister and hardly ever pays much attention to him. This sister, older by three years, is now very close to their mother but she is totally estranged from the patient. He speaks disparagingly of her whenever he can. In sharp contrast with his negative attitude, Aaron speaks lovingly about an older brother who recently passed away. He insists that his appraisals of the members of his family are accurate and based on a litany of either proper or improper treatments at their hands. He claims to be a fairly good evaluator of other people, but this supposed facility in empathic attunement is soon seen not to extend to a parallel one of empathic conduct. Thus there is to be no place for his saying that he is at a loss as to how to behave in any given situation, because he seems quite able, but not always willing, to act with understanding and tact. It is always a matter of choice.

Aaron's childhood was one of significant achievement and advance in school, and he tells of being ahead of everyone in just about everything he did. He was smarter, faster, cleverer than just about everyone else, and he now delights in recounting his exploits. School was a breeze and work was always a challenge that Aaron met. He not so secretly felt that he was better than everyone else at whatever he tried. He had no hobbies or outside interests. Aaron describes his father as someone equally shrewd and clever, but never healthy. The father had been ill as long as Aaron remembered and was thought of as being somewhat disabled for his entire life. Father walked with difficulty, was overweight and often short of breath, and certainly not able to participate in games with his sons.

The treatment with Aaron exemplified a familiar therapeutic narrative. It began with a common struggle over regularity with a number of cancellations and misses. After a certain stability was attained, we could connect his symptoms to disruption and his relief of them to the continuity of treatment. With this background in place, the transference began to take form with a characteristic set of mild reflections on the analyst's integrity, competence, and ability to see the world correctly. The debunking gave way, however, to a developing feeling of safety and security. Within this atmosphere of protection, Aaron felt remarkably contented and even a little sad. When and if the inevitable breaks or disruptions occurred in the transference, there would be an upsurge of the familiar grandiosity with its accompanying overbearing and offensive presentation. The sequence became clear: a fragile connection to an idealized parent that nonetheless lent itself to the characteristics of the ideal, the most prominent of which for Aaron was dependability. A disruption in this transference configuration inevitably led to a reawakened investment in the grandiose megalomania that warded off the anxiety following the feelings of being unprotected. No sooner would the connection be restored than the grandiosity would begin to dissipate, and shortly thereafter Aaron would look askance at this other self. Aaron then began to reflect on his divided self.

This example clearly signifies a more significant vertical split than the preceding one. It seems to come about regularly and predictably, rather than with the "out-of-the-blue" description of the previous example. It also seems to be more pervasive, more inclusive of the total personality, and a bit less foreign or alien than that of a limited dissociative state. Yet there still is a feeling that one wishes at times to be free of it and regrets its appearance. It is not, however, a carrier of a totally negative and dysphoric state and is more easily rationalized and even welcomed. The critical or disowning posture of the patient is, more often than not, seen after some time has passed and reflection is allowed to take place. This attitude of dislike is such a variable phenomenon that it soon becomes an important element or clue to the successful treatment of these patients. Whether one seeks therapy for this sort of personality disorder depends on a number of factors, including the depression that lurks in the background and that may make an appearance at times. There is a great deal of difference among patients in the recognition of this particularly unhappy state.

The place of the parental ideal in these two categories of patients has a similarity and a difference. The similarity is seen in an initial connection to a parental idealized other who is experienced as strong and supportive. This is the familiar omnipotence and omniscience that is indicative of this phase of development in the relation to the ideal parental imago. Jerome, our first patient, had a secure connection to relatively strong parents, and so his disillusionment did not overtake him to the degree that it did with Aaron. Aaron felt more radically dropped by a parent who could not offer him the strength that he needed. He went through life feeling unprotected and frightened, but compensated with a bombastic and overbearing presentation.

Aaron's conception of reality involved a powerful insistence on *his* way being the *right* way of seeing things. Other people, and particularly his therapist, were naïve and innocent. His intense conviction that he could and should rely only on himself was reinforced by dismissing alternative views of events. In these patients the move to eliminate or diminish the vertical split is more in the direction of a reluctant submission to another's opinion than the befuddlement seen in our first category of patients. It is not a question of having their feelings and perceptions justified, as in the first category of limited dissociation, but rather of allowing themselves to see a given situation in another way. To take the example of anger, Jerome must slowly embrace and accept it, whereas Aaron must consider giving it up, at least for a while. That is to say, that he more clearly recognizes his dual reality is untenable. He cannot insist on being enraged along with being tolerant. With the next category of patient we see this position of opposition to be even more striking and dramatic.

Case 3—Narcissistic Behavior Disorders

The previously-noted physician patient who behaved in an inappropriate and illicit way with patients is an example of a much more profound and obvious vertical split. Earlier it was noted that he too felt unprotected as a child, because his parents could not help him with his severe leg pain. Coupled with this failure was the inability of his mother and father to respond to other narcissistic needs such as mirroring and validation. He tells a story of receiving his acceptance to medical school and running in proudly to announce this exciting news to his mother, who was working in the kitchen. She turned to him and asked that he not raise his voice. He remembers running outside and screaming to the sky. Thus one can trace the connection to his later need to display his penis silently and never ask for help.

Rather than presenting a problem confined to, or predominant in, one pole of self-development, cases of behavior disorder seem regularly to have dual problems (i.e., in both grandiosity and idealization). For the most part, they have no doubt that their misbehavior survives in an alternate reality, and they do not usually spend much time or effort in justification of their conduct. In the first category, limited dissociation, the patient needs to recognize the split-off part; in the second category, narcissistic personality disorder, one needs to cease rationalizing and submit to what they seem to "know" as correct. In the third category of behavior disorder, most patients wish more or less to obliterate this parallel sector of alternative behavior. This suggested sequence thus has both quantitative and qualitative differences that move from sporadic dysphoria to more prevalent personality differences to overt misbehavior. With each of them the problem of reality is different, and in each the split is progressively more distinct and severe.

The dual problem in narcissistic behavior disorders may be studied to allow one to see how the behavior is sanctioned by a superego and ego ideal that have failed, along with a mirroring failure that has not properly allowed the self to be structuralized and develop adequate restraint. Thus the ideal has not failed in a single one of its tasks of predictability, reliability, and dependability but more probably in all three. The reconnection to the developmental failures in these cases involves enactments in more than a single form. The behavior has taken on a significant role in the amelioration of painful affects and in the effort to avoid further regression and disintegration. One may see the mirroring failure in either the misbehaving or the more organized sector, but there is no reasonable guide to its emergence. The most severe disorganization is no doubt seen in the reputed cases of multiple personality disorders.

Cases of Multiple Personality Disorder and the Question of "Many Minds"

It would seem that there is a natural progression from a single vertical split that offers two minds separate and apart to some version of many splits leading to multiple minds. The single most interesting preliminary point of entry to this sort of study is that some clinicians claim they have seen and examined quite a few such individuals; others insist that this syndrome is a myth and a fable. Ever since Prince (1905) introduced the idea of such a disorder, there has been a debate as to its authenticity. In recent years, the debate has ranged from Lowenstein and Ross (1992), who claim that multiple personality disorder involves a new paradigm in our thinking, to Spanos (1996) who insists that it is a product of the times and not a bona fide disorder at all. It certainly does capture the imagination of many authors (Hacking, 1998) outside of psychiatry, and it does seem to have a variable popularity. If one inquires of therapists who have never seen a single case, they may report that it never comes up, or else they quickly disabuse a patient, who insists on that diagnosis, of the probability of that idea. If one asks therapists who find the disorder rather regularly how they explain the discrepancy in the rate of its recognition, they report that one must be prepared to discover it or else it is missed.

Dennett (Humphrey and Dennett, 1998), a philosopher, surmised that multiple personality disorders might provide a clue as to whether there is an underlying continuity to human psychic structure. Working with a psychologist, Nicholas Humphrey, he studied the problem and interviewed a number of patients and therapists. The criteria the two authors listed for MPD to be real were:

1. The different selves would have different "spokesmen" with access to the memories and thoughts of one self to the other being the same as of the mind of one human being to the mind of another.
2. Each self will claim to have conscious control over the subject's behavior.
3. Each self will be convinced of its own rhetoric.
4. This self-rhetoric will be convincing to others.
5. Different selves will be distinctive.
6. The "splitting" into separate selves will have occurred before treatment.

The authors found that *no* case met these criteria, but they found a plethora of anecdotes. They concluded that a "candidate phenomenon" existed without any scientific proof (Humphrey and Dennett, 1998, p. 45). One may readily agree with them that the syndrome may be said to exist, but that this existence may well result from the treatment. As an aside, however, there is no doubt that these same criteria are regularly met in cases of vertical splits with but two minds, and that these seem not to be products of treatment.

Patients with multiple personality disorders are correlated with the supposed existence of "repressed memories." Eldridge (1997) states: "The dissociated content of memories and affect are not linguistically encoded; rather they are stored in confusing fragments of sight, sound, and touch accompanied by intense affective states. This form of memory is extremely painful to recall and creates the experience of fragmentation" (p. 72). This state of disorganization is also said to be a product of severe child abuse.

I cannot add anything to settle the debate about whether such pathology exists, but perhaps some insight from the study of behavior disorders will be of interest. The recent publication of a book by Mollon, who both believes in and treats patients with multiple personality disorder, presents cases in which he insists that the therapist must engage in action with the patient. Mollon claims that these patients have deficits, they need a new emotional experience with the therapist, and the regular crossing of boundaries ranging from hugging to entering into the trance scene of the abuse to modify the trauma is allowable as long as one understands the meaning of such behavior (Mollon, 1998).

I think it a mistake to automatically consider behavior to be primitive and so not "linguistically encoded." We live in language from birth (Nelson, 1996) and only the failure to recognize nonverbal communication and bring it into words gives one license to participate in the range of behaviors condoned and perhaps rationalized by so many therapists. Is it not possible that the presence of one or another of these personalities is a response to a signaling from the therapist? This is a common theme in the description of treatments after the existence of "alters" has been established. Lyon (1992) describes a patient who first talked about voices in her head and in subsequent sessions had her "alters" appear. I suspect that this would not have happened with a therapist who did not believe in multiple personality.

Spanos (1996) claims that the therapeutic interactions described in the treatment of these patients are often dramatic and go beyond the usual kinds of therapeutic work. There can be little doubt that such patients are disorganized, and that the therapist aids in a reorganization (Gottlieb, 1997). One must go beyond mere co-construction, however, for an explanation of the persons that appear in studies of multiple personalities, inasmuch as many of the contributions of the therapist may exist outside of his or her ken. As Humphrey and Dennett (1998) point out,

"Any interaction with a patient involves cooperation and respect which shade imperceptibly into collusion" (p. 48). They tell of the encounters with multiples having a "séance-like quality" to them. To this extent, cases of alleged multiple personality are continuous with our own findings on those cases of behavior disorder that manifest a blurring of reality and regularly invite a silent collusion.

The Common Underlying Depression

As noted earlier, one characteristic that seems to be fairly regularly found in all of these patients regardless of the particular group in which they fall is depression. If one takes a careful history, it is not at all unusual to hear of either a clearly demarcated period of depression that occurred much earlier in life or else a haunting background of depression that is kept at bay. Patients with behavior disorders seem able to move very quickly into action to ward off the depression, and treatment is regularly seen by them as an invitation (and so a warning) to become depressed. The early failures of treatment are often due to overzealous therapists who convey overoptimism. Patients with personality disorders are much better able to experience their depression in treatment, and it is occasionally seen as welcome in that it lends a certain feeling of authenticity to a person who may have felt fake and unreal for much of his or her life. Dissociated patients are much more familiar with depression and come closest to seeing it as a symptom and an intruder.

Thus, the different categories of split seem to manifest different aspects of depression. Some say it is an emptiness, some an aloneness, and some a terror that is disabling. The prudent use of antidepressants is often advisable in severe depressions that occur during treatment, and the possibility of suicide must be kept in the forefront of one's consideration. The literature on more severe cases of multiple splits seems to suggest a disorganization that is a derivative of fragmentation rather than of depression (Eldridge, 1997), but this remains an uncharted area. Caution in the use of hypnosis and other radical forms of treatment is therefore an absolute necessity lest one push a patient into a more severely regressive state.

After the Split Is Healed

Stern (1985) states that an integrated self encompasses attributes of agency, affectivity, coherence, and historicity. Shane, Shane, and Gales (1997) add to this definition the concept of a consolidated self that has the additional qualities of an intersubjective capacity, a sense of conviction of what is real, creative strategies, adaptive self-protective strategies, self-reflective strategies, and the achievement of a secure attachment or intimate tie to another. Healthy infants are said to achieve stable configurations or enduring patterns and develop the complex motivations that sustain them through life.

Patients with a vertical split do indeed manifest evidence of poor integration and consolidation of the self. One can readily see most if not all of the features of the unintegrated or unconsolidated self in practically all of the patients we have discussed. It may be unfair to impose one's own set of values on others, however, especially in those patients who seem reluctant to pursue the elimination of one or another of their supposed failings. It is not only a question of therapeutic ambition but also of appreciating what exactly another person desires in those qualities of integration and consolidation. Without in any way diminishing the attributes of an ideally cohesive self, it is usually the case that the healing of the vertical split yields some improvement in some of these features along with an absence of change in others. The process of treatment often involves discovering both what the patient wishes to ameliorate and what is feasible to change. This issue of workable compromising becomes the substance of the next chapter, which is an effort to characterize a different sort of split that exemplifies the field of psychoanalysis per se. The chapter begins with a caution about our therapeutic ambitions in, for example, our desire to have our patients achieve particular forms of intimacy. We need to expend an effort to reconcile these ambitions with both our own and our patients' limitations. To aim for an image of an integrated self that satisfies a preconceived concept of health may possibly be another, more subtle, version of a therapist's unacknowledged split. Just as a therapist must use caution in determining what is bad for patients, so too he must exercise caution in determining what is good for them.

Chapter 11

BETWEEN EMPATHY AND JUDGMENT

This chapter is designed to move away from the purely pathological manifestations of the vertical split to an examination of the
phenomenon of "being of two minds" as it lives in everyday clinical practice and, indeed, in the very way we live. Once again, this
configuration can be seen as consisting of unequal but separate
sectors, each of which forms one coherent set of goals and values
as distinct from the other. Although at times these sectors may be
seen in opposition, they are routinely set apart in a tension that
may seem to ask for a union. It is to the achievement of that
union that we may find some of the more creative moments in
psychoanalysis. I begin with a case that is offered for study to
examine this state of tension.

A patient of mine, whom I shall call Karl, said he wanted very
much to write a letter to Ann Landers or Dear Abby. He had come
to me after seeing several therapists preparatory to his "coming
out" as homosexual, and in each case these therapists were on
hand to aid him in reaching this decision. Because of my own
admitted uncertainty about what he "really" was, and for other
reasons based on my concern about his life apart from his avowed
sexuality, he decided to enter analysis with me. In the analysis, he
discovered that his homosexual fantasies were serving what were
essentially nonsexual purposes, and he soon became for the first
time rather actively heterosexual. He was overjoyed, while I myself
can only remember being somewhat relieved.

A friend of mine who is a gay therapist (i.e., someone who is himself gay and primarily treats gays), tells me that my patient is really heterosexual, and this is now what my patient claims, and it is just what he wants to tell the Lederer sisters. He wants them to know that one should never urge anyone to declare himself as gay or be directed to a gay therapist or take any such definitive steps until and unless he knows for sure. And so here is the crux of the matter. Karl says that his analysis allowed him to discover what he really was (i.e., he was able to know for sure). Without analysis, he might well have decided to become gay, and that possibility now offends him. He feels that he was very close to a terrible mistake. But interestingly, he feels that there are many other aspects of himself that are likewise what he really may be, or seems to be, or would like to be, and that he wishes to be made other than what is now the existing state of affairs. He would have liked his analysis to change these aspects for him as well. He wishes that he were more sociable; why hasn't his analysis helped him there? He feels he is somewhat lazy and now insists that analysis should and indeed could have made him more industrious. I wonder if he seems to be willing to discover and modify some things about himself—like his sexuality—and feel that these things are a mark of authenticity, while at the same time he comes upon other qualities—like a certain aloofness in relationships—and considers them only questionably authentic but eminently alterable. He agrees. But he cannot settle for analysis being confined to the mere unlocking of potentials. Is it not supposed to do more? Should it not only allow or enable us to be different but also make it so?

Karl thinks analysts feel that a patient is like an unlit Roman candle on the Fourth of July. The analyst lights it and steps to the side to watch and hopes to admire the display. Some Roman candles are splendid, and some are duds. Blame the factory. But surely one needs to take more responsibility for the display, because no one really seems to step to the side. Karl agrees that his own analysis could not be said to have been clearly weighted on the side of heterosexuality, but he always suspected that I had a bias in its favor. The neutral stance that I adopted was, in truth, more related to a personal confusion of mine than to a principled conviction. He and I shared a goal, and to say otherwise would be to hide behind a cloak of neutrality that seemed more transparent than real. Or so he says.

This variation on the nature-nurture argument has in the past had a rather clear solution in psychoanalysis. One part of the solution is that of real physical constraints. We cannot make people taller or shorter, but perhaps when it comes to weight, we are a bit less certain. As each piece of new evidence of the physical or biological makes its appearance, however, we tend to retreat. When we learn of the neurological basis of obsessive-compulsive disorder, we subsequently read the case of Freud's Rat Man with a different eye. When we become convinced of the genetic basis of bipolar disease, we begin to think less of the dynamic formulations once ascribed to it. But when this putative genetic factor is called into question, we quickly reclaim our psychological position. Thus we become prisoners of the latest and best physical basis of the psyches. And surely sexuality is bedrock—or is it?

The other guiding solution for what can and should be done for patients, and thus what is in the best interest of the patient, is our own set of standards and norms. These standards have become principles that tell us how people ought to be; and we work to get our patients as close to them as possible. We have all devised some set of developmental steps that we consider normal and therefore desirable. To travel along the correct path of development and reach a goal that we feel is optimal is the blueprint, whether secret or open, that we use to measure our patients. Thus, in our supposed willingness to have a patient find his or her own path of self-fulfillment, we also posit a map of knowing where exactly he or she should end up.

Sexuality and gender seem to be, or should be, easy. For a while there, everyone had to be heterosexual. Of late psychiatry and (reluctantly) psychoanalysis have moved to a clear espousal of normal homosexuality. At each of these poles there seems to be a pathology as well, that is, there exists a pathological heterosexuality that covers over or defends against a variety of painful situations up to and including homosexuality. So the situation was and is getting more complex. We regularly see heterosexually promiscuous or deviant men or women who struggle against homosexual intimacy, just as we see gay promiscuity defend against heterosexual closeness. At one point in his treatment, Karl said that he might have gone either way, and so one surely has to consider bisexuality as yet another variant of normal sexual orientation. Is it really the case that psychoanalysis allows one to determine what one really is without the analyst also making some determination? Is it possible that there is no such thing as what one really "is"?

In an excellent review based primarily on Ogden's version of Kleinian thinking, Sweetnam (1996) argues for gender being dialectical and therefore fixed at certain times and fluid at others. She claims that different psychological positions—the paranoid and the depressive—provide a context for the anxieties, defenses, object relationships, subjectivity, and symbolization that alter the quality of gender experience. These "positions" organize experience. The paranoid and the depressive positions provide a context that goes beyond the linear developmental timetable or the comprehension of singular identifications. Sweetnam's aim is to balance the biological determinism ascribed to Freud with the newly popular cultural determinism of other investigators by proposing a framework that embraces both fluidity and firmness. The essential point of that effort is to see our psychology as constrained or perhaps trapped between biology and culture, between the body and the world.

At any point and at any moment we seem to make some judgment of the way things ought to be, and we begin to direct the process according to that judgment. It is a judgment based on what we claim to be correct and true and real. But just as biology seems to help at certain times, so cultural factors seem to weigh in at others. There can be little doubt that people can go more than one way in more than one domain. It seems at times a bit naïve to say that we really let the patient decide, or that we merely allow normal development to unfold. We are not merely watching. After we relinquish our neutral stance as untenable, however, we are still committed to stand somewhere. Lest we too quickly claim an allegiance to the newly popular embrace of "authenticity," we should probably recognize that one can be an authentic scoundrel as well as a saint. Where once we felt that we need be only empathic with our patients, we find that we cannot help but judge them as well. Sometimes these tasks seem to be at odds and in need of a unity. And so we must now consider the reconciliation of our empathy and our judgment.

Two Perspectives

At the outset I should like to clarify some of the basic positions I see as fundamental to psychoanalysis. It is first and foremost a psychology that is devoted to what some philosophers and many scientists have called a first-person perspective that centers on the view of the world from a subjective sense (i.e., that which says I know, I see, I experience). The opposing viewpoint is the third person—that which is objective, external, and makes statements about him or her or it that sees, knows, and experiences. First-person perspectives are available to introspection, to conscious personal scrutiny and assessment, and are said by some to be incorrigible (i.e., uncorrectable) because one is, or should be, the sole determinant of a personal experience. On the other hand, a third-person perspective is available to objective and public examination and testing, and is the clear winner in a scientific tug-of-war. To complete the picture, we consider a second-person perspective, the experience that *you* are having as graspable by another by way of an inner comparison or vicarious introspection. The sad fate of psychoanalysis is the ever-present temptation to adopt tempted by a third-person perspective as some ultimate goal of achievement. Most neurophysiologists lay claim to a third-person perspective as allowing a complete description and explanation of any and all brain phenomena and so being the goal of all studies of behavior. But most, if not all, scientists also agree that first- and third-person psychology are and shall remain irreducible, that is, there can be no reduction of all first-person psychology into third-person psychology. There can be no elimination of the "I" experience. Biology and social psychology can never replace depth psychology. They remain complementary but distinctive perspectives.

It is worth a moment to justify this thesis of the irreducibility of first- and third-person perspectives, because there is an ever-present and recurring effort to treat depth psychology as a way station to some sought-for biosocial final explanation. Psychoanalysis becomes wedged in between biology and social psychology in a true scientific effort to explain all there is to know about people from an objective point of view. But just as no study limited to the makeup of DNA (i.e., the genetic code) can reveal the final genotype, so too the study of neuronal pathways demands an experience to say just what is the fate of this or that brain activity. When we know just how and why the brain produces the color brown, we still need to determine exactly what color is experienced. Nor should we be fooled into thinking that knowing enough about the brain will close a gap that exists for both empirical and conceptual reasons. No matter how much we may and do subscribe to the premise that all phenomena are ultimately neural, as they surely are, we need to recognize with equal certainty that psychological phenomena are not thereby eliminated from consideration. In truth, a recent statement by an eminent perceptual physiologist states: "Perceptual findings must be considered primary, and if the neurophysiological data do not agree, the neurophysiological data must be wrong" (Uttal, 1997). The first-person perspective is essential. Our subjective experience can never be eliminated and so carries a claim to correctness.

On the other or social side of the ledger is the recent accumulating evidence that calls into question the biological innateness of sexuality, especially for women who seem to be capable of choosing their sexual identity (Golden, 1997). Research seems to reveal that some women who identify themselves as bisexual find that they are able to entertain possibilities of choosing to be lesbian or heterosexual. Biology seems to fade in the presence of powerful social and cultural factors. Still, the limits of the fluidity of sexuality are underscored by the reports of that ridiculous experiment by Money (*Chicago Tribune*), who advised parents to raise a boy whose penis had been accidentally amputated as a girl. After countless surgeries and hormone treatments, the child finally insisted on becoming the boy that he knew he was. One may theorize that biology or early imprinting were factors here, but I suspect that an analytically informed observer could see that simply everyone around the child knew that he was a boy masquerading as a girl and the communication of that fact, albeit nonverbally, was omnipresent. Again we see that sometimes biology seems to rule the day and sometimes social factors seem to predominate. But a first-person psychology remains, in spite of whatever third-person issues are studied and raised, because only such a perspective allows entry into the personal experiences of the subject. The sole reliance on a first-person perspective, however, regularly raises problems that continue to trouble our field.

The temptation to plant psychoanalysis on what was felt to be a firmer, more scientific ground certainly began with Freud in his *Project*, but it was later championed by Heinz Hartmann, who insisted that psychoanalysis was an "explaining" rather than an "understanding" psychology. Hartmann said that the study of forces in opposition, of energy and its expression, was the scientific ground of psychoanalysis. For him, "understanding psychology" is necessarily unreliable and so fails to be a true causal science. Only an explanation of the causal relationships in the mind can bring psychoanalysis to its rightful place in science, and these causal connections are not inferred on the basis of reports of subjective experience, but rather signify (in his words) the actual mental connections. Empathy is not only filled with potential errors but neglects that part of our personality—the unconscious—that is fundamental to psychoanalysis. Hartmann wanted psychoanalysis to be objective and thus able to be seen as reliable and capable of validation. He essentially pleaded for a third-person psychology. He felt that our judgments or truths were clearly objective and so must rule.

The love affair of analysis and objectivity was certainly cooled, if not shattered, by the central role assigned to empathy in psychoanalysis by Heinz Kohut and his colleagues. Although the two Heinzes were social friends, ideologically they were quite far apart. The concentration on empathy as vicarious introspection moved psychoanalysis back to a first-person perspective. This focus has been taken up by countless derivatives or variations on the theme, from an insistence on seeing things primarily from the patient's point of view to embracing a postmodern or relativist position that brings into question the very existence of truth or fact or objectivity. Things are what they are felt to be and not what others say they are. What happened to the patient as a child is not a question of history but of meaning. The Kurosawa film *Rashomon* becomes the new cultural symbol of psychoanalysis, and our recent conferences highlight "it all depends" as an introductory mantra. To see the world from the perspective of the patient is to suspend judgment and, perhaps momentarily, to enjoy a trial identification with the other.

A problem that presents itself in any singular focus on empathy is that it is either a sustained or a momentary inquiry into a conscious experience. When one steps into the shoes of another person to introspect vicariously, just as one might personally turn to one's inner world, the material available to introspection is, by definition, conscious. That is, first-person perspective entails experiences that have qualities and are realized by our feelings. We own our experiences, and they are a conscious part of us. Imagine the difference between a name that you cannot remember and one that you cannot possibly have known. The first is felt as something that must be brought back into our awareness, whereas the second has no ownership claims and remains outside of our selves unless and until it becomes known and conscious. Therefore the whole role and place of the psychoanalytic unconscious becomes problematic for those who limit clinical data to the empathically accessible.

To be sure, the complex role of empathy in psychotherapy and psychoanalysis is not diminished by a recognition of its inherent limitations. But we need to add a crucial component to the data that are obtained by empathy. It is a component that belongs to the observer and it may be thought of as consisting of preconceptions, perspectives, or theories, but it is essentially derived from the eye of the empathizer. It is a judgment. The balance to the purely subjective experience of the patient is offered by the judgments brought by the observer. These are his theories, his preconceptions, his morality. If he believes in the unconscious, then he adds it to the mix. To gain access to another we carry ourselves and our beliefs along, and so every first-person perspective, every study of individual meaning, becomes seen and then changed by the onlooker. (And it perhaps needs to be said that every objective or third-person perspective also carries with it the subjective coloration of the observer.) The psychoanalytic observer, the empathic student of a patient, carries her convictions and judgments not only about the patient's reported experiences but also about what is said to be known, at first, only to the analyst: the content of the patient's unconscious. Initially this is felt as foreign or separate by the patient. The unconscious is not experienced as first-person phenomenon. It is alien and apart and to bring it into subjective experience, to realize Freud's "Where id is, there ego shall be"—what was once regarded as the work of psychoanalysis—is to make the supposed third-person perspective of the contents of the unconscious, however we may conceptualize them, into the first-person perspective of subjective ownership and individual meanings. The two Heinzes must be joined in the reconciliation of empathy and judgment.

The autobiography of the analysand is "since Rousseau a construction, not a representation" (Bernstein, 1995), and it is formed by the introduction by the analyst into what she or he knows and presumes is present, primarily if not exclusively, in the patient's unconscious. These additions are the shifts or switches between facts and meanings, objective and subjective, judgment and empathy that we all live with as we understand our patients while we simultaneously judge them. We should emphasize that empathy or understanding or first-person psychology is certainly not opposed to judgment or explanation or third-person psychology; rather, the two interpenetrate one another. The same has been said for creation, erroneously limited to artistic endeavors, and discovery, falsely limited to the scientific domain. The argument about psychoanalysis as either art or science is on the same erroneous basis, that is, it assigns to separate domains what are actually endpoints on a continuum. To fault one's empathic approach by noting its contamination with inferences is the same as condemning one's objectivity by seeing the subjective component in it. These are conceptual errors. Empathy and judgment must penetrate one another as do discovery and creation. Because analysis is a first-person psychology, however, we need to see it as what one writer has termed "a theory-mediated autobiography" (Bernstein, 1995, p. 70). In this way we find that many theories, from Freudian to Kleinian to Kohutian to Lacanian, can be used to achieve an acceptable redescription of childhood and indeed of all personal experience. They are all true, because the formation of the biography becomes shaped by those who create it. The coauthored autobiography that emerges from a psychoanalysis is a first-person account of a life written by two people. It is an empathic account interpenetrated by the judgments of the other. It is the best illustration imaginable of the integration of a split, of the necessity of being of two minds that can, nevertheless, connect.

Clinical Implications

To better see psychoanalysis as a first-person psychology requires some clinically relevant material. My patient Karl was a voyeur who would periodically and regularly find himself looking at men's penises in locker rooms and masturbating with the immediate memory of it. Karl hated himself for doing this and spoke of its occurrence as if it belonged to someone else, as if he would not and could not own it. He had a split in his self that seemed to allow the coexistence of parallel personalities with different sets of goals and ambitions, different values and needs, indeed seemingly different sets of psychic organization. And as we have seen, usually one self is acknowledged and the other despised (i.e., one is understood and the other is harshly judged). That both aspects or personalities are conscious is no clear answer to the problem of the split. One is me and the other is him.

In speaking of repression, which Kohut later termed the horizontal split, Freud (1910) said:

> It is a long superseded idea, and one derived from superficial appearances, that the patient suffers from a sort of ignorance, and that if one removes the ignorance by giving him information (about the causal connection of his illness with his life, about his experiences in childhood, and so on) he is bound to recover. The pathological factor is not his ignorance in itself, but the root of his ignorance in his inner resistances; it was they that first called this ignorance into being, and they still maintain it now [p. 225].

But the split of disavowal (first noted by Freud [1927] with the fetishist) is vertical rather than horizontal, and here the patient both knows and yet does not acknowledge, just as would happen if the contents of the unconscious were made known to the patient and were therefore conscious but not really owned or experienced as part of the self. It is thus again not a matter of ignorance but of an attitude of abhorrence about what is known. We have seen how these patients judge themselves; it is not like those who suffer guilt from a harsh superego. Rather, they treat themselves as other persons whom they would prefer to shun; they see themselves from a third-person perspective and so disown a part of themselves.

We usually note that the anxious or depressed patient is, on one hand, *unable* to step aside from his or her symptom and so disavow it. On the other hand, Carol, our earlier patient, spoke of her binges as if she very much, in retrospect, disliked that person who stuffed herself with Oreo cookies. And in treatment the therapist or analyst more often than not joins with the patient in this harsh judgment. The college professor who steals books in an unpredictable and uncontrollable manner very much expects the analyst to be as critical of his behavior as he is. Save for those individuals whose behavior disorders dominate their psyches, patients with vertical splits always live a life poised between understanding and judging and ask the same of their analyst. Indeed, their treatment becomes a virtual laboratory for a study of the tension between empathy and judgment. The psychoanalyst shares the split of the patient as she or he struggles to understand and *not* condemn, while almost simultaneously being asked to condemn until she can perhaps understand. When one treats a scoundrel, be it a thief, liar, voyeur, or addict, it is foolhardy to claim a neutrality for oneself. We always take a stand. And some of us, in turn, judge ourselves harshly or benignly for the stand that we take.

Perhaps one of the more interesting phenomena that have emerged in a group of analysts who discussed these points is the wide range of tolerance (or intolerance) claimed by those analysts who made up our investigating group. Whereas one of us may be quite content to have a stalker as a patient, another may be totally unable to sustain a therapeutic stance toward such behavior. The analyst who comfortably treats a thief is considered to be himself mildly unusual but only by some members of the group—until that moment in our discussions when he betrays his own corrupt self. And when that moment occurs, he is as astonished as anyone to see himself as a kindred soul to his dishonest patient. The movement from tolerant understanding to critical judgment becomes a routine feature of our group discussions, with some members resting more easily in one phase than another. The dishonesty of one of our analysts is sharply attacked and condemned by the others until, over time, we begin to see the lack of purity and inherent contradictions that we all possess. What were sharp lines of demarcation between right and wrong, truth and falsehood, and especially degrees of moral judgment, shade into vague domains of personal opinion. We seem unable to find a stable resting place as we shift between the parallel selves of our patients and discover shades of the same split in the shadow of our own selves.

The transition from the one perspective to the other is graphically demonstrated by the Lacanian, Zizek, who describes the story of a serial killer in the movie *When a Stranger Calls*. He talks of the killer, first as an unfathomable object with no identification, and then describes the sudden transposition into the perspective of the killer himself. The author discusses the two points of view: that of the victim and that of the murderer, and the sudden twist of the movie. He says: "The entire subversive effect hangs upon the rupture, the passage from one perspective to the other, the change which confers upon the hitherto impossible/unattainable object or body, which gives the untouchable thing a voice and makes it speak, in short, which subjectivizes it" (Zizek,

1992). Once captured by the identification with a murderer, we find it difficult to depart from that position and once again objectify and inevitably despise him. We are necessarily denied the comfort that we previously had of knowing for sure. I think that that comfort is best thought of for all of us as a warning, because the true interpenetration of empathy and judgment makes for the unstable state that is more proper to the life of a psychoanalyst. We do, however, manage to carve out positions of resolution, and those positions partake of both the judgmental condemnation suggested to us by Freud in his consideration of the endpoint of analysis and the state of self-empathy that is needed to restore balance to our ever-present condition of uncertainty and lack of closure. Our resolution maintains the interpenetration of judgment and empathy.

Empathy, Judgment, and Treatment

Let us consider empathy as, more or less, discovery, and judgment as creation. Moving back and forth between empathy, which aims to discover what is there but sometimes is not accessible, and judgment, which creates something by bringing in new material is, as we have noted, both a paradox and a sought-after state. The autobiographies that we create are necessarily shaped by the theories that we employ (i.e., by our judgment) to mediate what we hope to discover in our patients by way of empathy. We discover by using our theories what is in the unconscious, but we actually accomplish these discoveries by our knowing beforehand what is or can be found. Similarly, our patients recognize the split-off area, either vertical or horizontal, as really belonging to them. In that way, the foreign territory of both the repressed and the disavowed, the psyche split off vertically and horizontally, needs to be joined with the rest of the psyche. In our patients with behavior disorders, we are able to be empathic first with one side, then with the other, and ultimately with both. We must realize, however, that seeing things exactly as the patient does makes blind men of us both. We need to remain objective about our subjectivity; we always judge or evaluate our meanings as we step aside and see ourselves as we would see another.

This oscillation between empathy and judgment has a counterpart in our consideration of just what we find in a patient versus what we bring to our investigations. With Karl, I knew that I wanted to rid him of his voyeurism, but I could also rather easily identify with that activity; I was more puzzled than anything about his both embracing and repudiating his homosexual longings. Over time I became convinced that they represented a sexualization related to the transference. And so I brought my judgment into his analysis and created a new configuration.

The history of technique in psychoanalysis has been a journey from discovery to creation. The first pioneers in the field were intent on discovering the contents and makeup of the unconscious. The myriad present-day interactive theories deal with the mutually created products of analytic and therapeutic work. And many contemporary investigators seem to want to resolve the dilemma by some sort of fifty-fifty compromise of parity. No one any longer seems to deny the import of the analyst. Nor is anyone likely to say that the patient's past and unconscious are not to be reckoned with. Unfortunately, the resolution often seems to be effected by a popularity poll, and more often than not tends to become generalized to apply to all of our patients. But what I have learned from Karl and so many others is a simple truth that sometimes I matter and sometimes I do not. I may matter when I wish I did not, and when I really wish that I would matter, it often has come to naught. It is different with every patient, just as I myself am different with each of them. One might even say that Karl found what he wanted in me: that peculiar combination of being able to understand as well as judge him, a combination that differed enough from his own makeup to allow for a change but was close enough to enable a connection. With perfect empathy he would have had no chance, and with unrelenting judgment he would have had no space.

Behavior disorders are striking in their appeal to our individual judgments because of the existential and moral issues that so dominate their study. That moral concern exists, however, to some extent in every treatment we conduct. It is regularly concealed within our theories and our particular views of what we consider to be right and proper, normal and expectable. This particular form of psychopathology regularly evokes a moral judgment in us, but every form of psychopathology calls forth a variety of beliefs or opinions that are essentially what Gadamer called our prejudices (Warnke, 1987). There is no way that we can see a patient without our preconceptions and prejudices, but they do not equally affect all patients. For some patients, empathy dominates the treatment; others seem to be most attuned to our individual input in the form of our personalities and our theories. Contemporary psychoanalysts run the risk of attributing either too much or too little to their presence and thereby losing sight of individual patients' varying needs. We must always focus on the first-person perspective, which obliges us to consider the impact of our input on the patient, but the great need of future psychoanalytic research is to determine more accurately which patient has the significance of the therapist as a central concern and which finds it peripheral. We cannot discount the possibility that the idea of our significance may be another variety of prejudice. Being empathic surely must mean to be able to judge what we mean and what we have brought to our patients. Our input should neither be disregarded nor made too much of.

The biological and physical constraints or limitations of ourselves and our patients alike become joined with their subjective experience along with the culture in which we find ourselves. The necessary interpenetration of first- and third-person perspectives makes for a continual reassessment of any particular bit of analytic data. There are no pure forms; equally, there are no fixed percentages of input. Sometimes biology matters a lot and sometimes a little. The same can be said of sociocultural factors and especially of our own contributions as analysts. Co-construction does not imply equal partners. Transference does not mean that we are just doing our jobs with no ulterior motive. Perhaps this built-in level of uncertainty is what makes psychoanalysis so interesting.

A final antinomy that bedevils our field is one that most psychoanalysts find especially obnoxious: the supposed contradiction that exists between history and fiction. Since Freud, we have been urged to liken ourselves to archeologists who unearth the hidden, and we do so in the most careful and cautious effort to avoid disturbing the past or contaminating the relics. But these relics are but traces of the past, and they demand an imaginative interpretation to allow us to see, in one scholar's words, "what I would have witnessed, if I had been there" (White, 1978). When we devise these imaginary mediations (Ricouer, 1988), we begin to interweave fiction and history and so we form our reconstructions according to one type of preferred story rather than another. This fictionalization of history allows us to construct at times a tragedy, at other times a comic novel. We begin to write our own imaginative interpretations of what is remembered as history but is recast as a moment in the present (Monk et al., 1997).

One very common psychoanalytic event is the retelling of particular significant episodes from a patient's childhood. Each recall carries with it a new possibility of reinterpretation and perhaps a new and better understanding. For Karl, there was the momentous time after his parents' divorce when his father came to take him and his sister out for the weekly parental visit. This historical event, in which Karl feigned sleep so as not to join his sister, became the nucleus of a whole set of scenarios. Sometimes Karl hoped for his father to return for him alone. Sometimes Karl would have time alone with his mother. Sometimes Karl would give up his act and race to join his father and sister. As analyst, I would imaginatively revisit the scene and silently write the script that I hoped was history as represented but knew was being newly written as a fictionalization of history. Yet another integration becomes a part of our life and work.

Once again we see the interpenetration of history and fiction as we did with the first- and third-person perspective, with discovery and creation, and with empathy and judgment. The inevitable mix, however, is not tantamount to contamination. Each perspective is enriched by the other.

Summary

Karl himself provided the answer to his lament, when he came to see me shortly before his marriage and some months after his official termination. It is apparent to any analyst who has listened to this tale that my patient's complaint, which introduced this chapter, revolved around that remaining bit of transference directed to the parent who had failed to be perfect and to make his son Karl perfect. He told me that he still occasionally wanted to look at men, but that was something he could manage and live with. His gratitude to me and to his analysis was properly tempered with the disappointment that must accompany any treatment. I was pleased and a little hurt, but found comfort in recognizing that analysis, both as a profession and as an individual encounter, is a very mixed bag.

Chapter 12

TRYING ON ANOTHER MIND

I am afraid that this may be seen as an old-fashioned book. It uses traditional and somewhat out-of-date ideas about psychological defenses and structure, transference and countertransference. In particular, it focuses on the concept of disavowal and its many other names. It is strikingly neglectful of new ideas coming out of neurophysiology, cognitive science, interpersonal and intersubjective relations, and motivational theory (Shevrin 1997). Mainly it talks about the mind, and here one is forced *not* to equate the mind with the brain, because surely the title *Being of Two Minds* cannot be equated with being of two brains. As Barbara Herrnstein Smith (1998) has observed, "The mind may be seen as a name given to a shifting set of heterogeneous phenomena and notions, ranging from observable patterns of behavior and introspected experiences to the various faculties and interior mechanisms that, at various times and in various informal and formal discussions (philosophical, ethical, legal, medical and so forth) have been posited or assumed to explain them" (p. 3). If we think about this quote we can see that one may explain some bit of behavior as being right or wrong, or true or false, and clearly be speaking of the mind. In the same manner one can introspectively contemplate the very same issues and attribute that mental activity of contemplation as well to a function of the mind. It is all just as easily described as products of the brain, but the discourse is different, and one does not "explain" mental activities by pointing to the brain. Rather, we simply change the subject. In doing so we may rob ourselves of a chance to understand these activities. As clinicians, we rarely enrich ourselves by engaging in that debate, so it is to the mind that we must turn.

The other problem with this book is that of the self. Whereas some may say that the self or the person (and even that equation can begin a heated discussion) is composed of the body plus the mind, others, such as William James, extend the concept of self beyond the skin, to include, for example, one's possessions. People are socially embedded and cannot be lifted away as discrete objects of study. Both the mind and the self are placed in a system of organization without which they cannot exist. One's individuality or singularity is therefore not denied, but is seen as a result of positioning of that separatedness in relation to its ecosystem. That positioning becomes the basis of my supposed neglect of interpersonal and intersubjective terminology. It is not that these ideas do not have a proper place in describing social phenomena, but rather that my preferred language and theory (i.e., what I resort to in explaining the embeddedness of the self) is that of the selfobject and self psychology. The linkage of the self to the larger system, from this purview, takes place by way of its constituent selfobjects. This linkage returns us to old-fashioned ideas of transference and countertransference, and so this study deals primarily with the selfobject transferences. It does not dismiss or banish the viewpoint of noting what goes on between and within the shared space of persons. Rather, it chooses as its focus the psychoanalytic concern with unconscious transference material. And here once again comes the out-of-vogue vocabulary of psychic structure, defenses, and most especially the almost worn-out term of disavowal.

Sometimes called denial—always a focus of theoretical worry about just what it consists of—disavowal becomes a major tenant in the structure that we choose to construct. That the exchange between patient and therapist is a co-constructed one is no longer a matter of contention. Nor do we argue about whether the contributions of the two participants are equal. But the emphasis on transference and countertransference is underscored here to remind us that the therapeutic program is that of the patient who extracts what is needed from the therapist. The latter may insist on things being otherwise or may override the patient's direction, but that venture is misguided; it does not make for a preferred "intersubjective" or "interpersonal" point of view or perspective. Rather, it should return our concern to that of the patient as center of the treatment. This view is illustrated by the case material in this book, because we have posited that a split in the patient is often met and matched by a split in the analyst. Together they maintain the disavowal and are, inevitably, each of two minds. The therapist or analyst is, however, not offering this up to the patient as an undertaking of mutual construction; rather, the experience is more like that of being invited to meet and match the patient's pathology. That co-construction is something formed by both, but always according to the blueprint of the patient. To shift the fundamental stance of analytic treatment to a dialogue or to liken it to a conversation certainly balances the disparity between patient and therapist, but it may also invite us to notice elements that are unimportant at times while failing to attend to those that are most significant (Arlow, 1979). We study the vertical split that originates in childhood, expresses itself in adulthood, and emerges in treatment. We do not study the co-constructed vertical split that is formed by the intersection of patient and therapist. The latter split must be seen as a derivative, and to this extent our concern with the interpersonal or intersubjective derives from the patient's psychology, or, better said, it is the patient's autobiography that we must write. We are sometimes slow to realize that we are actors in this script, and we often do not take kindly to our assignments.

Case Illustration

A therapist comes to a supervisor with the complaint that nothing seems to be happening in his treatment of a woman who has been seeing him for several years. The patient is a socially prominent person who is carrying on an illicit affair with a man with whom she insists she can never be seen in public. Not only would her marriage be jeopardized if she were to be seen with this person, but the notoriety would be equally damaging to her status and position in society. Their meetings are furtive and planned to avoid disclosure. This is not the first such affair that she has conducted. An entire series of such affairs has been rationalized on the basis of the lack of fulfillment in her married life. Her psychotherapy had seen this pattern as a minor theme.

Her therapist reports his hours with her to the supervisor and his efforts to learn more about these secretive relationships. He matter-of-factly notes that he has arranged for this patient to both arrive at and leave his office by way of a separate door at clearly designated times so that she need not be seen in the waiting room. He feels that he is in full agreement with her insistence that it would be much to her detriment if she were seen by anyone who recognized her as coming to see a therapist. When this parallel furtiveness of the patient's affair and the manner of arriving and leaving the office is pointed out to this therapist by his supervisor, he is clearly stunned by its obviousness and by the similarity of words used to describe both the treatment and the infidelity. It clearly did not seem to qualify as something that he did not know, although he would claim that he did indeed both know and not know. Nor would he possibly claim that this was not something that was co-constructed by him and his patient. But he would probably also insist that it is not something that he does or has done with anyone else. It is under the patient's direction that he is an unwitting actor. This seems to fit with the concept of transference without in any way diminishing the relevance of co-construction and intersubjectivity, but the latter do not exist alone.

Back to Our "Two Minds"

Although analysts and therapists have little difficulty in noting the disavowal that operates in their patients, they react with surprise and dismay at its existence in themselves. When Freud discussed the reluctance of people to tolerate the existence of the unconscious, he said it was because it forced them to admit that they were not masters in their own psychological household (Freud, 1917). Over the years there have been a number of variations on this theme as psychoanalysis has struggled to know and thus master the unconscious, and Kohut (1984) has discussed how we have juxtaposed knowledge with mastery and raised knowledge to its exalted position in psychoanalytic theory. There is no doubt that something similar to our comfort in our knowing occurs in our personal experience with the reciprocal splits with our patients, but often a few more unpleasantries seem to confront us.

The most striking uncomfortable states for therapists are those found in the behavior disorders, and one may begin these descriptions with the chagrin of the preceding case wherein the therapist felt mainly foolish at colluding with his patient in allowing his patient to enter and leave by way of a separate door. This mild surprise is the easiest with which to contend. As one encounters patients who live lives of deviance, the issue of collusion becomes more prominent. It seems to be unavoidably true in all of our cases that a therapist must be able to allow the emergence of the disavowed sector by way of his or her "touch" of the same deviance. Thus we not only have to confront the injuries that Freud cautioned us to recognize, those offered by Copernicus and Darwin. We must now enlarge or expand the narcissistic injury that Freud attributed to the contents of our unconscious, that is, that we are ignorant of the contents of our mind. We are, however, not ignorant of these activities but merely choose or are forced to disown them. That condition forces us to move from a picture of innocence to one of responsibility. When we first see a patient who misbehaves, we often or at least ideally begin by not taking sides. As we become empathic with our patient, we temporarily suspend a judgmental stand—but it is only in suspension. We may subsequently wish to join with the patient's own harsh stand toward that sector of misbehavior, but our present-day position on that maneuver once again insists that we can only help that patient if we can be as culpable as is he. That entry into the sector of misbehavior, be it stealing or lying or perverse activity, enables us to recognize its existence alongside the need of the patient to disown it. Only by knowing it can we connect it to the judgmental part.

The surprise and the shame that crop up seem to combine to insist that that behavior is none of ours. My friend who treats the supermarket thief tells me that he could not enter into that aberrant sector of his patient and her mind and so I conclude that he never could truly be with her. My colleague who condoned extramarital affairs in his patient could too readily join his patient in that "forbidden" life, and so he was unable simultaneously to brand it as deviant, because that would require him to step aside. He could not tolerate that judgment of himself. But perhaps more upsetting than this struggle with shock and self-criticism is the simple but overwhelming fact that there may at times seem to be two of us. Many of my friends and colleagues who hear of this inevitable necessary parallel split insist that it is only an occasional event, and even then primarily occurs in other therapists.

Some even take pride in their failures to treat thieves or incest perpetrators and point to this as a badge of rectitude. How can one possibly present a successfully treated case of a scoundrel to one's colleagues without a confession of some measure of reciprocal sinfulness? These therapists insist that there must be exceptions, that it need not always be the case, that more work is needed. They do not recognize that stranger beside them. They feel that they surely know their own mind.

In a book entitled *The Fabric of Reality* (1997) the theoretical physicist David Deutsch puts forth the suggestion that there are parallel universes, that is, worlds similar to our own that coexist with the one in which we find ourselves. I am by no means competent to judge the truth of what he says, and my first reaction to his well-supported conclusion was that it was nonsense. Deutsch makes his claim based on some very well described and irrefutable experiments that are simply unexplainable. That is, they are unexplainable until the proposition of our universe not encompassing all of reality is entertained and a multiverse is presented as the solution. As I struggled with the absolutely absurd idea that such could be the case up to and including another Arnold Goldberg writing a different (and better) book in another universe, I began to recognize a familiar feeling. It is a feeling of *not* wanting to know, all the while claiming that I certainly do want to know. That is the feeling of our patients who disavow, along with our fellow clinicians who make a claim for truth and reality. They know their mind, and it is but one. A parallel mind is out of the question. The very necessary antidote to that awful malady of certainty is the presence of wonder. Of course, I know that there is but one universe, and I can observe it and study it and ultimately know it. But . . . I wonder.

REFERENCES

Arbib, M. A. & Hesse, M. B. (1986), *The Construction of Reality.* Cambridge, UK: Cambridge University Press.

Arlow, J. (1971), Character perversion. In *Currents in Psychoanalysis,* ed. I. W. Marcas. New York: International Universities Press, pp. 317–336.

———— (1979), The genesis of interpretation. *Journal of the American Psychoanalytic Association,* 27:193–206.

Basch, M. F. (1983), The perception of reality and the disavowal of meaning. *The Annual of Psychoanalysis,* 11:125–154. Hillsdale, NJ: The Analytic Press.

———— (1988), *Understanding Psychotherapy.* New York: Basic Books.

———— (1995), *Doing Brief Psychotherapy.* New York: Basic Books.

Bateson, G. (1972), *Steps to an Ecology of Mind.* New York: Ballantine Books.

Bernstein, J. M. (1995), *Recovering Ethical Life.* London: Routledge.

Bion, W. R. (1962), *Learning from Experience.* New York: Basic Books.

Block, N. (1995), On a confusion about a function of consciousness. *Brain and Behavioral Science,* 18:227–287.

Bollas, C. (1987), *The Shadow of the Object: Psychoanalysis of the Unthought Known.* New York: Columbia University Press.

Bowlby, J. (1980), *Attachment and Loss, Vol. 3.* New York: Basic Books, pp. 44–74.

Bremner, J. D. & Marmar, C. R. (1998), *Trauma, Memory, and Dissociation.* Washington, DC: American Psychiatric Press.

Brenner, C. (1979), Working alliance, therapeutic alliance, and transference. *Journal of the American Psychoanalytic Association,* 27(Supplement):137–158.

Breuer, J. & Freud, S. (1893–1895), Studies on hysteria. *Standard Edition,* 2:40–309. London: Hogarth Press, 1955.

Coates, S. W. (1977), Is it time to jettison the concept of developmental line? *Gender and Psychoanalysis*, 2:35–53.

Coleridge, S. T. (1817), *Biographia Literaria*, Chapter 14.

Cummings, R. (1989), *Meaning and Mental Representation*. Cambridge, MA: MIT Press.

Davidson, D. (1991), What is present to the mind. In *Consciousness*, ed. E. Villanueva. Atiscodero, CA: Ridgeview Publishing, pp. 197–313.

Deutsch, D. (1997), *The Fabric of Reality*. New York: Allen Lane.

Eldridge, A. (1997), Walking into the eye of the storm: Encountering "repressed memories" in the therapeutic context. *Conversations in Self Psychology, Progress in Self Psychology, Vol. 13*, ed. A. Goldberg. Hillsdale, NJ: The Analytic Press, pp. 69–71.

Ferenczi, S. (1913) Stages in the development of the sense of reality. In *Selected Papers, Vol. 1*. London: Hogarth Press, 1955, pp. 213–239.

Fortune, M. (1994), Therapy and intimacy: Confused about boundaries. *The Christian Century*, June 1–8.

Freud, A. (1936), *The Ego and the Mechanisms of Defense*. New York: International Universities Press, 1953.

Freud, S. (1900), The interpretation of dreams. *Standard Edition*, 4/5. London: Hogarth Press, 1953.

——— (1905), Three essays on the theory of sexuality. *Standard Edition*, 7:130–243. London: Hogarth Press, 1953.

——— (1910), Observations on "wild" analysis. *Standard Edition*, 11:219–227. London: Hogarth Press, 1957.

——— (1917), Introductory lectures on psycho-analysis. *Standard Edition*, 16:243–463. London: Hogarth Press, 1963.

——— (1927), Fetishism. *Standard Edition*, 16:149–158. London: Hogarth Press, 1961.

——— (1940), Splitting of the ego in the process of defence. *Standard Edition*, 23:275–278. London: Hogarth Press, 1964.

Gabbard, G. (1995), The early history of boundary violations in psychoanalysis. *Journal of the American Psychoanalytic Association*, 43:1115–1136.

——— (1994), Psychotherapists who transgress sexual boundaries with patients. *Bulletin of the Menninger Clinic*, 58:124–135.

Gedo, J. & Goldberg, A. (1973), *Models of the Mind*. Chicago: University of Chicago Press.

Gill, M. (1979), The analysis of the transference. *Journal of the American Psychoanalytic Association*, 27(Supplement):263–288.

Goldberg, A. (1988), Self psychology and external reality. In *A Fresh Look at Psychoanalysis*. Hillsdale, NJ: The Analytic Press, pp. 61–73.

——— (1995), *The Problem of Perversion*. New Haven, CT: Yale University Press.

Golden, C. (1997), Do women choose their sexual identity? *The Harvard Gay and Lesbian Review*, Winter:18–20.

Goldstein, W. N. (1991), Clarification of projective identification. *American Journal of Psychiatry*, 148:153–161.

Goodman, N. (1978), *Ways of Worldmaking*. Indianapolis, IN: Hackett.

Gottleib, R. M. (1997), Does the mind fall apart in multiple personality disorders? *Journal of the American Psychoanalytic Association*, 45:832–907.

Grossman, L. (1993), The perverse attitudes to reality. *Psychoanalytic Quarterly*, 62:422–436.

Hacking, I. (1998), *Rewriting the Soul: Multiple Personality and the Science of Memory*. Princeton, NJ: Princeton University Press.

Heidegger, M. (1966), *Being and Time*, trans. J. Stambaugh. Albany: State University of New York Press.

Heyward, C. (1993), *When Boundaries Betray Us: Beyond Illusions of What Is Ethical in Therapy and Life*. New York: Harper Collins.

Hoffman, I. (1991), Toward a social-constructivist view of the psycho-analytic situation. *Psychoanalytic Dialogues*, 1:74–105.

Humphrey, N. & Dennett, D. C. (1998), Speaking for our selves. In *Brainchildren: Essays on Designing Minds*, by D. C. Dennett. Cambridge, MA: Bradford.

Jacobs, T. J. (1994), Nonverbal communication: Some reflections on their role in the psychoanalytic process and psychoanalytic education. *Journal of the American Psychoanalytic Association*, 42:741–762.

James, O. (1998), *Britain on the Couch*. London: Century.

Johnson, A. & Szurek, S. (1952), The genesis of antisocial acting-out in children and adults. *Psychoanalytic Quarterly*, 21:323–343.

Jones, E. (1957), *The Life and Work of Sigmund Freud, Vol. 3: The Last Phase 1919–1939*. New York: Basic Books.

Kantrowitz, J. (1996), *The Patient's Impact on the Analyst*. Hillsdale, NJ: The Analytic Press.

Kohut, H. (1971), *The Analysis of the Self*. New York: International Universities Press.

———— (1984), *How Does Analysis Cure?* ed. A. Goldberg & P. Stepansky. Chicago: University of Chicago Press.

LaPlanche, J. & Pontalis, J. B. (1967), *The Language of Psychoanalysis*, trans. D. Nicholas-Smith. New York: Norton, 1973.

Levin, F. M. (1991), *Mapping the Mind: The Intersection of Psychoanalysis and Neuroscience*. Hillsdale, NJ: The Analytic Press.

Litowitz, B. (1998), An expanded developmental line for negation, rejec-tion, refusal, and denial. *Journal of the American Psychoanalytic Association*, 46:121–148.

Lothstein, L. M. (1997), Pantyhose fetishism and self cohesion: A para-philic solution. *Gender and Psychoanalysis*, 2:103–119.

Lowenstein, R. & Ross, D. (1992), Multiple personality and psycho-analysis: An introduction. *Psychoanalytic Inquiry*, 12:3–48.

Lyon, K. A. (1992), Shattered mirror: A fragment of the treatment of a patient with multiple personality disorders. *Psychoanalytic Inquiry*, 12:71–94.

Marcus, D. M. (1997), On knowing what one knows. *Psychoanalytic Quarterly*, 66:219–240.

Massie, H. & Szajnberg, N. (1997), The ontogeny of a sexual fetish from birth to age 30 and memory processes. *International Journal of Psychoanalysis*, 78:755–771.

Mollon, P. (1998), *Multiple Selves, Multiple Voices: Working with Trauma, Violation and Dissociation*. Chichester: Wiley.

Monk, G., Winslade, J., Crockett, K. & Epston, D., eds. (1997), *Narrative Therapy in Practice: The Archaeology of Hope*. San Francisco: Jossey-Bass.

Montaigne, M. (1588), *Essays*. Boston: Houghton Mifflin, 1902–1904.

Moore, B. & Fine, B., eds. (1998), *Psychoanalytic Terms and Concepts*. New Haven, CT: Yale University Press.

Natsoulas, T. (1978), Consciousness. *American Psychologist*, 33:906–914.

Nelson, K. (1996), *Language in Cognitive Development*. Cambridge, UK: Cambridge University Press.

Palombo, J. (1997), Nonverbal communication in psychotherapy: Diagnostic considerations. A disorder of the self in an adult with a nonverbal learning disability. Unpublished.

Penot, B. (1998), Disavowal of reality as an act of filial piety. *International Journal of Psycho-Analysis*, 79:27–40.

Piaget, J. (1954), *The Construction of Reality in the Child*, trans. M. Cook. New York: Basic Books.

Piatelli-Palmarini, M., ed. (1980), *Language and Learning: The Debate Between Jean Piaget and Noam Chomsky*. Cambridge, MA: Harvard University Press.

Prince, M. (1905), *The Dissociation of a Personality: A Biological Study in Abnormal Psychology*. New York: Longman, Green.

Proust, M. (1933), *In Search of Lost Time, Vol. 3: The Guermantes Way*, trans. C. K. Scott-Moncrieff & T. Kilmarte. Revised by D. J. Enright. New York: The Modern Library, 1981, p. 80.

Psychiatric News (1997), Vol. 32(17), September 5.

Rangell, L. (1979), Contemporary issues on theory of treatment. *Journal of the American Psychoanalytic Association*, 27(Supplement):81–112.

Reed, G. S. (1997), The analyst's interpretation as fetish. *Journal of the American Psychoanalytic Association*, 95:1153–1181.

Reich, W. (1933), *Character Analysis*. New York: Orgone Institute Press, 1945.

Renik, O. (1992), Use of the analyst as a fetish. *Psychoanalytic Quarterly*, 61:542–563.

——— (1996), The perils of neutrality. *Psychoanalytic Quarterly*, 65:495–517.

Ricoeur, P. (1988), *Time and Narrative, Vol. 3*. Chicago: University of Chicago Press.

——— (1992), *Oneself as Another*, trans. K. Blainey. Chicago: University of Chicago Press.

Rosenblatt, A. D. (1997), The analyst's reality. *Journal of the American Psychoanalytic Association*, 45:395–406.

Sandler, J. (1960), The background of safety. *International Journal of Psycho-Analysis*, 91:352–356.

Searle, J. R. (1995), The construction of social reality. New York: Free Press.

Shane, M., Shane, E. & Gales, M. (1997), *Intimate Attachments*. New York: Guilford Press.

Shevrin, H. (1997), Psychoanalysis as the patient: High in feeling, low in energy. *Journal of the American Psychoanalytic Association*, 45:841–864.

Smith, B. H. (1998), Is it really a computer? Review of Steven Pinker's *How the Mind Works: Times Literary Supplement*, February 20. p. 3.

Spanos, N. P. (1996), *Multiple Identities and False Memories: A Sociocognitive Perspective*. Washington, DC: American Psychological Association.

Spitz, R. (1957), *No and Yes: On the Genesis of Human Communication*. New York: International Universities Press.

Stern, D. N. (1985), *The Interpersonal World of the Infant*. New York: Basic Books.

Strean, H. S. (1980), *The Extramarital Affair*. New York: The Free Press.

Sullivan, H. S. (1953), *The Interpersonal Theory of Psychiatry*. New York: W. W. Norton.

Sweetnam, A. (1996), The changing contexts of gender: Between fixed and fluid experience. *Psychoanalytic Dialogues*, 6:437–460.

Thelen, E. & Smith, L. B. (1994), *A Dynamic Systems Approach to the Development of Cognition and Action*. Cambridge, MA: MIT Press.

Trevarthen, C. (1982) The primary motives for cooperative understanding, in *Social Cognition: Studies of the Development of Understanding*, ed. G. Butterworth & P. Light. London: Harvard University Press, pp. 77–109.

Uttal, W. R. (1997), Do theoretical bridges exist between experience and neurophysiology? *Perspectives in Biology and Medicine*, 40:280–302.

Verghese, A. (1998), The pathology of sex. *The New Yorker*, February 16, p. 47.

Vygotsky, L. (1986), *Thought and Language*, ed. A. Kozulen. Cambridge, MA: MIT Press.

Warnke, G. (1987), *Gadamer: Hermeneutics, Tradition and Reason*. Stanford, CA: Stanford University Press.

White, H. (1978), *The Tropes of Discourse*. Baltimore: Johns Hopkins Press.

Winnicott, D. W. (1960), Ego distinction in terms of true and false self. *The Maturational Processes and the Facilitating Environment*. New York: International Universities Press, 1965.

Zizek, S. (1992), *Enjoy Your Symptom: Jacques Lacan in Hollywood and Out*. New York: Routledge.

INDEX